BRITAIN'S PLANT GALLS

A photographic guide

compiled by
Michael Chinery
for the British Plant Gall Society

First published in Great Britain in 2011 by WildGuides Ltd.
Reprinted with amendments 2016.

Copyright © 2011 The British Plant Gall Society.

Copyright in the photographs remains with the individual photographers.

ISBN: 978-190365743-0

Production and Design by **WILD**Guides Ltd., Old Basing, Hampshire.

Printed by Drukarnia Dimograf, Poland.

Contents

The plant galls described and illustrated in this book are arranged in three major groups according to their host plants.

The first group deals with galls on oak trees. These may well be the first galls to come to the notice of the general naturalist, for they include some of the commonest and most conspicuous of our plant galls.

The second group covers the galls on trees and shrubs other than oaks, while the third group deals with galls on herbaceous plants.

Within the second and third groups the host plants are generally arranged in alphabetical order of their English names.

The index of host plants will simplify the task of tracking down galls on particular hosts.

Unless otherwise indicated, the description of each gall is to the left or right of the illustration.

Biologists are continually learning more about the relationships of plants and animals, and scientific names are continually being changed to reflect these relationships. Many of the scientific names given in this book therefore differ from those appearing in older books, including the first edition of this title.

The robin's pincushion, caused by the gall wasp **Diplolepis rosae**, is the emblem of the British Plant Gall Society.

Introduction

The oak marble galls pictured *right* and the robin's pincushion galls (*facing page and p. 59*) that perch on wild rose bushes are well known to most people with an interest in natural history and the countryside. Some people will be familiar with other plant galls, such as the nail galls that develop on lime leaves (*see p. 50*), without necessarily knowing what causes them, but it will probably come as a surprise to most to learn that we have about 2,000 different kinds of galls in the British Isles. They occur on a wide variety of woody and herbaceous plants and also on many fungi, lichens, and algae. Although most galls are small and inconspicuous, some display beautiful colours and bizarre designs, and these are not difficult to find. It is hoped that this book will allow the naturalist to identify some of the commoner and more conspicuous of our galls and also to learn a little about them.

Marble galls on oak, caused by the gall wasp **Andricus kollari**.

So what exactly are these strange lumps and bumps that we call galls, and what causes them? Much has been written in recent years concerning the definition of a plant gall and by no means all cecidologists – the smart word for those naturalists who study galls – are agreed on a definition even now, but the generally accepted definition is that a plant gall is an abnormal growth induced by the presence of another organism

*Galls induced by bacteria are solid, irregular masses of tissue without any obvious organisation. **Agrobacterium tumefaciens** is one of the commonest gall-causing bacteria, using hundreds of different woody and herbaceous species as hosts, although it rarely attacks grasses or other monocotyledons. Galls of this kind, commonly known as crown galls, often develop around wounds. The photograph shows a huge crown gall on a birch trunk, but most crown galls are a good deal smaller than this.*

living in or on the host plant and causing its cells to enlarge and/or multiply to provide *both food and shelter* for the gall-causer. The latter is therefore essentially parasitic, although few gall-causers seem to cause more than localised, short-term damage to their host plants. Most gall-causers stick to one host species or a group of closely related species.

Plant galls can be caused or induced by a very wide variety of organisms, including bacteria, nematodes or eelworms, and even other plants, but most of our galls are caused by insects, mites, or fungi. Although we do not know exactly how the galls are initiated, it seems clear that most gall-causers interfere with the development of the host plants' cells, either chemically or mechanically, and cause them to develop into gall tissue. Closely-related gall-causers are often very difficult to distinguish, but they can induce very dissimilar galls, even on the same plant, as a result of differences in their actions, and there are few better examples of this than the diverse maple galls induced by mites of the genus *Aceria* (*see p. 51–52*).

Mistletoe is a semi-parasitic shrub that grows on a variety of trees. It can photosynthesise its own food but draws water and minerals from its host through specialised roots (haustoria) that penetrate the host's vascular system and cause distinct swellings. Thus the mistletoe is clearly a gall-causer, although its galls are usually concealed under its evergreen foliage.

Gall-causing Fungi

The fungi that induce galls are very small organisms, with little similarity to the more familiar mushrooms and bracket fungi that we see in the countryside. They are commonly called micro-fungi, although some of them induce quite large and often bizarre growths on their host plants – one of the strangest being the tongue-like gall protruding from female alder catkins (*see p. 32*). Most of our gall-causing fungi are either smuts or rusts. Smut fungi, named for the powdery black spores produced by most species, attack a wide range of herbaceous plants, although relatively few of the hundred or so British species actually induce galls. Several smuts attack flowers, causing the anthers or ovaries to swell and become filled with sooty spores. The maize smut (*see p. 76*) is one of the most striking examples.

Rust fungi are named for the rust-coloured spore-bearing patches that develop on their host plants. There are about 260 species in the British Isles and they attack a wide range of both woody and herbaceous plants, although they do not

The anthers of this soapwort flower have been galled by the smut **Microbotryum saponariae**, with the pollen replaced by a mass of sooty spores.

The underside of this lady's mantle leaf is more or less completely covered with the aecia of the rust fungus **Trachyspora intrusa**.

all induce galls. Several rusts cause serious plant diseases. The rusts probably have the most complex life cycles of any organism, with up to five different spore-producing stages. Unlike the smut fungi, many rusts require two different host species for the completion of their life cycles.

Although some rust fungi exhibit all five spore-bearing stages during their life cycles, many species have omitted one or more stages and only two kinds of spore-bearing structures need concern the gall-hunter. The most commonly seen stage among the gall-causing rusts is the aecium or aecidium (plural aecia or aecidia). Individual aecia are very small, but they form dense aggregations and are responsible for the orange or rust-coloured patches on the host plants. Most aecia appear cup-shaped when magnified and they are sometimes referred to as cluster cups. Notable exceptions include the aecia of various *Gymnosporangium* species, which take the form of small spikes (*see p. 61*). Whatever their form, the aecia scatter wind-borne aeciospores (or aecidiospores) that germinate as soon as they reach suitable host plants.

The other main spore-bearing stage of the gall-causing rusts is the telium (plural telia), which tends to appear in late summer or autumn. It scatters spores known as teliospores or teleutospores and in most rust species these are resting stages, often remaining dormant through the winter and starting the cycle again in the following spring. The telia and their spores are often dark brown or black. Many rusts are capable of initiating gall formation in both aecial and telial stages, sometimes on the same plant and sometimes on different host species, although some gall-causing rusts exhibit only one or the other of these stages.

Gall-causing Invertebrates

Insects and mites are the most abundant of the cecidogenic (gall-causing) invertebrates, and the gall wasps of the family Cynipidae are probably the best known of the gall-causing insects, although not all of the 90 or so British species actually induce galls: many are inquilines in the galls of other species (*see p. 12*). Only distantly related to the familiar garden wasps, the gall wasps are actually more like ants, only a few millimetres long and usually black or brown. Some species have both winged and wingless forms (*see p. 13*). The thorax is usually strongly domed and the abdomen is generally compressed from side to side. Most of the British and European species are associated with oaks, although some induce galls on roses and a few herbaceous plants, especially members of the daisy family. Eggs are laid in various parts of the host plant but, as with most gall-causers, gall-formation is initiated only when the larvae begin to feed. Pupation takes place inside the galls.

Many flies, belonging to several widely separated families, induce plant galls, with most of the gall-causers belonging to the family Cecidomyiidae. These are the gall midges – tiny insects mostly with brown or orange bodies and dark, rather hairy wings. Their antennae resemble miniature strings of beads. They induce galls in numerous woody and herbaceous plants and the larvae of many species jump when disturbed. Some gall midge larvae pupate in their galls, but most species leave their galls to pupate in the ground.

Andricus corruptrix *is a typical gall wasp* (×8).

Dasineura odoratae, *a typical gall midge* (×9).

Urophora cardui, *a typical gall-fly* (×5).

*Adult psyllids (**Trioza alacris***) and waxy nymphs exposed in a galled bay leaf*
(see p. 34) (×6).

The well-named picture-winged flies of the family Tephritidae are also known as gall-flies because several of them induce galls, although most of these galls are completely concealed in the seed heads of the host plants. The most familiar galls in the British countryside are the swellings in the stems of creeping thistle caused by the larvae of *Urophora cardui* (*facing page and p. 87*).

Psyllids (*pictured above*) are tiny sap-sucking bugs related to the aphids. Adults are always fully-winged and their hind legs are modified for jumping. Several species induce galls, the most obvious of which are leaf-rolls on various trees and shrubs. The insects cause the leaf margins to swell and roll up to create their living spaces. The galls may contain many insects and, unlike those of flies and gall wasps, the psyllid galls contain both adults and young.

Aphids are winged or wingless sap-sucking bugs that induce galls on a very wide range of plants. Their galls range from little more than crumpled leaves and leaf rolls to the complex pouch galls of poplar (*see p. 55*) and the pineapple galls of spruce (*see p. 67*) Adult insects settle on the plants and their feeding stimulates the formation of the galls. Many aphids can live and breed in a single gall, usually accompanied by copious waxy secretions, clearly visible in the opened poplar gall on the right. Life cycles involve both sexual and asexual forms, the latter giving

Pemphigus spyrothecae *aphids in a poplar petiole gall (×4).*

9

birth to active young. Some species require two different host species for the completion of their life cycles.

Sawflies belong with the gall wasps in the order Hymenoptera and get their name because in most species the female has a tiny saw-like ovipositor with which she cuts slits in plants prior to laying her eggs. Unlike other galling insects, she injects a stimulant when laying her eggs and the galls start to grow before the eggs hatch. Most sawfly galls are solid at first and usually contain a single larva that gradually hollows them out (*see p. 65*). Mature larvae of most species leave their galls before pupating – often in the soil.

Pontania proxima, *one of several similar gall-causing sawflies* (× 2·5).

A typical **gall mite** <u>very</u> *highly magnified.*

Gall mites have elongated bodies and just four tiny legs at the front end and they look more like maggots than typical mites. Visible only under high magnification, they cause a wide variety of gall forms, including pimples and leaf rolls. Most gall mites belong to the family Eriophyidae.

Galls can be found on any part of a plant – from the roots right up to the fruits and seeds – although most gall-causers stick to one or two areas of the host. Galls on the stems and leaves are obviously the most visible and familiar examples. The galls themselves differ enormously in shape and complexity. Among the simplest are the many mite-induced felt galls (*below left*). Also known as erinea, these occur mainly on the undersides of leaves and are basically patches of enlarged, often glassy hairs among which the mites live and feed. Other fairly simple galls include swollen

Felt galls are clusters of modified hairs. Pale at first, they usually darken with age.

Leaf roll gall of the aphid **Hayhurstia atriplicis** *on common orache.*

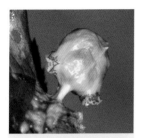

This 'fig gall', induced on an elm leaf by the aphid **Tetraneura ulmi** (see p. 42), is an entirely 'new' structure unrelated to any normal plant organ.

This 'knopper gall' growing on an acorn is caused by the gall wasp **Andricus quercuscalicis** (see p. 21) and is clearly a 'new' structure.

This oak artichoke gall, caused by the gall wasp **Andricus foecundatrix** (see p. 16), is clearly a modified bud, complete with much enlarged bud scales.

stems and the rolled-up leaves or leaf margins (*facing page*), induced by mites and assorted insects, notably aphids and the larvae of various flies. These galls usually contain a number of causers feeding in a single cavity.

The most intricate of our galls are those induced by the gall wasps. Many of these galls, notably the 'rose sputnik' gall (*see p. 60*) and the various oak spangle galls, are entirely 'new' structures, bearing no obvious similarity to any part of the host plant, while others are clearly modified buds or other normal structures. The galls

A mature, woody robin's pincushion gall, sectioned to show its numerous (vacated) larval chambers.

*A typical female **chalcid** parasitoid exhibiting her long ovipositor.*

of many of our gall wasps contain several distinct chambers, each containing a single grub. Such galls are known as multilocular galls and the robin's pincushion or bedeguar gall (*see p. 11*) is a good example. Galls with just a single chamber are equally common and are called unilocular galls.

Inquilines and Parasites

Although plant galls may contain numerous causers – the so-called rightful inhabitants – these are not the only creatures to be found in the galls and one cannot assume that an insect emerging from a gall actually caused it. Many gall wasps induce no galls of their own but lay their eggs in the galls of other species. Their grubs benefit from the food and shelter found there and, although they do not harm the gall-causers directly, by competing for the food supply they can starve them to death. These 'lodgers' are known as inquilines. Quite a few flies have similar life styles. Parasitic species, which include many, often brightly coloured chalcids (*see above*), actually feed on and kill the rightful occupants of the galls. The female parasite tends to have a long ovipositor with which she penetrates the galls to lays her eggs in or on the host grubs. Strictly speaking, these insects should be called parasitoids because typical parasites do not kill their hosts. Parasitoids also attack the inquilines, and a large gall, such as an oak apple, can house a very large insect community, consisting of dozens of individuals of several different species. Galls containing parasitoids or inquilines are commonly stunted or distorted.

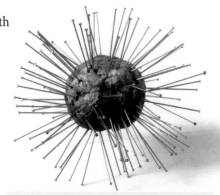

This oak apple contained at least 112 insects: each pin marks an exit hole.

Oak Galls

Our two native oaks – the pedunculate oak (*Quercus robur*) and the sessile oak (*Quercus petraea*) – together with their very common hybrid, support a great many galls and the introduced Turkey oak (*Quercus cerris*) also plays host to a fair number. Between them, these oaks support over 50 different galls in the British Isles. Most of these galls are caused by gall wasps (*see p. 8*) and they can be found on all parts of the tree, from the roots to the catkins and acorns. Most of our oak gall wasps have complex life cycles that involve the alternation of sexual and non-sexual (asexual or agamic) generations. Insects of the agamic generation are all females and they can lay fertile eggs without mating. A few species are known only in the asexual stages, although the sexual stages may be discovered one day. Apart from the agamic generations of *Biorhiza pallida* and *Trigonaspis megaptera*, which are wingless, all our gall wasps are fully winged and the generations can then be hard to distinguish.

Their galls, however, are often very different (see *Biorhiza pallida* on *p. 23*). The sexual and agamic generations commonly develop on the same tree, although *Andricus kollari* (*see p. 17*) and several of its close relatives produce their agamic galls on our native oaks and their sexual generations on the Turkey oak. All species pupate in their galls.

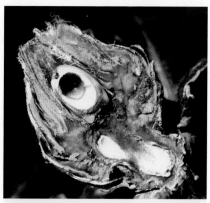

The artichoke gall (see p. 16) is one of several oak galls in which the grub lives in an inner chamber (exposed here in section).

Several species of oak gall wasps have been extending their ranges westwards across Europe in recent years. This is not a new phenomenon – the knopper gall (*p. 21*) and the cola nut gall (*p. 18*) appeared in Britain in the 1960s – but things do seem to have speeded up in the last 20 years, two of the latest arrivals being *Neuroterus saliens* (*see p. 26*), first noticed in 2004, and *Andricus gemmeus* which was discovered only in 2008. Climatic change may have something to do with it, but it seems more likely that big increases in trade and personal travel have contributed to the spread of these small insects, which are easily carried in produce and in vehicles. It is interesting that most of these newcomers rely on Turkey oak for at least one of their generations.

Agamic galls of **Andricus gemmeus** – one of the newer members of the British gall wasp fauna on oak.

13

The well-named ram's-horn gall is caused by the equally well-named gall wasp *Andricus aries*. The gall has a globular base and typically has two curved green or yellowish 'horns'. The latter are generally 2–3 cm long, but occasionally longer and sometimes much shorter – especially when the gall has been attacked by inquilines or parasitoids (*see p. 12*). The horns are sometimes fused into a single strap.

The gall develops from a bud during the summer and is green at first, but becomes brown and woody as it matures in the autumn. Adult gall wasps emerge in the autumn or in the following spring but the old galls (*bottom*) often remain on the trees for several years. A relative newcomer to the British Isles, *Andricus aries* was first discovered in Britain, in Berkshire, in 1997, but now inhabits most parts of England. Only the sexual generation is known at present.

These much-modified buds are the galls of the asexual generation of the gall wasp *Andricus corruptrix*. Up to 5 mm across, the galls are hard and woody and each one has up to five smoothly rounded lobes. Galls appear in late summer, but do not mature until July of the following year, when the adult insects emerge. These insects then fly to Turkey oaks and lay their eggs in the buds. Galls of the sexual generation sprout from the buds in late winter. Pale green at first, they soon become tinged with pink and then turn orange-brown as they mature in March. Mature sexual galls are egg-shaped with a pointed tip and about 2·5 mm long. They resemble the sexual galls of *A. kollari* (*see p. 18*), but there is normally just one gall in each bud.

The sexual generation of the gall wasp *Andricus inflator* causes the tips of the young twigs to swell in the spring. The galls are green at first, but soon take on the normal twig colour. Each gall encloses a tubular cavity, at the bottom of which is an egg-shaped inner gall containing the young gall wasp. Adult insects emerge during the summer, but the empty galls remain visible for years and growth often continues normally beyond them. After mating, the new females lay their eggs in the oak buds, leading to the development of ....

.... the asexual galls in the autumn. These globular galls are green and not very conspicuous at first, although they are very common on young twigs, especially on those that sprout directly from the trunk. Up to about 6 mm across and partly surrounded by bud scales, each gall contains a single larva. The galls gradually turn brown, and in late autumn they fall to the ground. The larvae pupate in their galls and the adults normally appear in the following spring, although some individuals spend two or even three winters in their galls before emerging to lay eggs in the young twigs.

The asexual generation of the gall wasp *Andricus foecundatrix* is responsible for the well-named artichoke or hop gall, which is a greatly enlarged bud, up to 30 mm long. Deep among the bud scales there is a hard, egg-shaped inner gall containing a single larva (*see p. 13*). Galls appear in mid-summer and mature in August, when the inner gall is forced out and falls to the ground, leaving just the dried scales on the twigs. Pupation takes place in the fallen galls and adults emerge in late spring to lay their eggs in the male flower buds. Galls of the sexual generation are inconspicuous, hairy swellings on the catkins.

These swellings are the vacated galls of the sexual generation of the gall wasp *Andricus curvator*. The galls appear soon after the leaves open and are often clustered near the leaf base, where they can cause severe distortion. Galls may also occur on young twigs and cause marked bending.
Each swelling has a small, egg-shaped inner gall in which the insect develops. The adults escape in May or June and the females lay their eggs in new buds, leading to the formation of the asexual galls (*below*).

Sometimes known as 'collared bud' galls, the asexual galls of *Andricus curvator* develop in young oak buds during the summer and mature in the autumn. They are concealed among the bud scales at first and very difficult to spot, but the scales may fall away later and expose the galls. Up to 3 mm long, each gall is smooth, brown, and skittle-shaped, with a nipple-like tip usually surrounded by a pale ring, although this ring is often indistinct in old galls. Although the galls mature in the autumn, the new adult gall wasps do not emerge until the spring and some may remain in their galls for a further year or two.

The gall of the asexual generation of *Andricus quadrilineatus* is one of the commoner galls on male oak catkins in the spring although, with a length of only 3–4 mm, it is rarely noticed. The galls are stalkless, with a distinctly ribbed or wrinkled surface, and change from green to red as they mature. In common with several other catkin galls, they cause the catkin stalks to thicken and to remain on the twigs for longer than normal. The galls fall in May or June, but the adult insects do not emerge until the following spring to lay their eggs in the opening buds. Galls of the sexual generation also develop on the male catkins, although they have not yet

been recorded in Britain. They are smaller and smoother than those of the asexual form and have hairy apices. This generation matures extremely quickly and lays its eggs on the same catkin crop, with the asexual galls appearing a few weeks later.

The marble gall, one of the most familiar of all galls, is caused by the asexual generation of the gall wasp *Andricus kollari*. This is not a native species, having been introduced early in the 19th century as a possible source of tannin for the dyeing and ink-making industries. The galls are now common all over the British Isles. Solitary or developing in small clusters, the galls are much modified buds, green at first (*below left*), but gradually turning brown and woody (*below right*). Up to 25 mm in diameter, each gall contains a single *A. kollari* larva, although many

inquilines and parasitoids may move in. The galls mature and most adult insects leave in the autumn, although the galls may remain on the tree for years. The asexual females leaving the galls seek out Turkey oaks and lay their eggs in the buds. The sexual generation arising from these eggs induces the development of tiny pointed, egg-like galls that poke from the buds in late winter or early spring (*right*). These galls are pale green at first, but soon become yellowish brown – after possibly developing a pink flush. The galls are between 2 and 3 mm long, often curved and shaped like miniature bananas. There are usually several in a bud and they mature in March, when the escaping adults mate and the females lay eggs in the buds of the native oaks to initiate another generation of marble galls.

Cola nut galls, caused by the asexual generation of the gall wasp **Andricus lignicolus**, resemble marble galls but are rarely more than 15 mm in diameter – and have a much rougher, scaly surface. Usually growing in small clusters, the galls are greyish when they first appear during the summer, but they turn brown as they mature and become extremely hard. Adult insects emerge in early autumn and lay their eggs in the buds of Turkey oaks, where the resulting larvae induce the formation of tiny egg-shaped galls up to 3 mm long. These are purple in the winter, but turn pale brown in the spring (*inset*). They resemble the sexual galls of *A. kollari* and *A. corruptrix* but have smoothly rounded tips. Adults of the sexual generation emerge in March.

The asexual generation of the gall wasp *Andricus sieboldi* is responsible for these galls growing on an oak sapling. Often called barnacle galls, they most commonly develop at or just below ground level, especially on saplings that have been damaged by grazing or mowing. Usually cream or purple when young, each gall is about 5 mm long and encloses a single *A. sieboldi* larva. The larva takes two or three years to mature, by which time the gall is hard and woody. Adult insects emerging in the spring lay their eggs in the opening leaf buds and the resulting larvae induce small, oval swellings in the mid-ribs or petioles. These swellings are the galls of the sexual generation, but they are rarely noticed until the adults have chewed their way out and left conspicuous exit holes. These sexual galls have not yet been recorded in the British Isles.

The 'hedgehog gall', induced by the asexual generation of the gall wasp *Andricus lucidus*, develops on buds and acorn cups in late summer and autumn. Up to 25 mm across, the gall bears hundreds of spines, each of which has a globular tip. The spines are sticky at first, but dry out as the gall matures. Each gall contains several larvae. Adults emerge in winter or early spring and lay their eggs in Turkey oak buds, leading to the development of the sexual generation, whose galls are pictured below. A fairly recent arrival, *A. lucidus* was first noticed in the London area early in the 1990s. Although still largely confined to the southern counties, it has recently been found in Yorkshire.

Galls of the sexual generation of *Andricus lucidus* develop in conspicuous, flower-like clusters on the male catkins of Turkey oak in late spring. They are greenish yellow at first, but become chestnut coloured when mature. Each cluster may reach 35 mm in diameter and contain dozens of individual galls that are basically dish-shaped although usually distorted by their neighbours. Each gall has two larval chambers at the base. The galled catkins remain on the trees until well into the summer, at which time the adult insects emerge and move to the common oaks where the mated females lay their eggs in the buds or on the developing acorn cups, leading to the development of the asexual hedgehog galls.

The asexual generation of the gall wasp *Andricus grossulariae* induces galls resembling the hedgehog galls of *A. lucidus*, albeit with flatter and less pin-like spines. Galls occasionally develop on male catkins (*above middle*), but usually occur on buds and acorn cups (*above left*). They are green at first, but tend to become purplish red later. Each gall has several chambers, each containing a single gall wasp larva. Adult insects emerge in winter and early spring and lay eggs in Turkey oak buds.

Galls of the sexual generation of *Andricus grossulariae* develop in large clusters on the male catkins of Turkey oak and resemble bunches of currants (*above right*), although each gall has a prominent point. Young galls are bright green, waxy, and slightly hairy. They ripen in late spring and become smooth and shiny and take on a deep maroon colour before becoming hard and woody. The adult insects emerge in June and July, although the galls may remain on the trees until the autumn. A newcomer, first found in the British Isles in Berkshire in 2000, the gall has spread rapidly and can now be found as far north as Yorkshire.

The asexual generation of the gall wasp *Andricus solitarius* is responsible for this skittle-shaped gall – a modified bud growing between two normal buds. The insect is well-named, for it is rare to find more than one gall in one place. Up to 10 mm long, the gall is clothed with rust-coloured hairs when it first appears in early summer, but becomes smooth later. Adult insects emerge in the autumn or in the following spring. Eggs are laid in dormant buds and they lead to the development of inconspicuous hairy galls on the male catkins in the spring.

The knopper gall, induced by the asexual generation of the gall wasp **Andricus quercuscalicis**, develops on acorns. It is roughly conical and often strongly ridged or knobbly. A terminal opening leads to a large cavity containing an egg-shaped inner gall. Two or more galls may develop on a single acorn and completely conceal it. Green and sticky at first, the galls often take on a reddish tinge as they mature, and then become brown and woody. Galled acorns fall from the

trees in late summer and the adult insects normally emerge in the following spring, although some may remain in their galls for up to four years. They lay their eggs in Turkey oak buds and the resulting larvae – the sexual generation – induce tiny cone-shaped galls on the male catkins. The knopper gall arrived in Britain in the 1960s and caused great alarm for a while because of the widespread destruction of the acorn crop but, although it is extremely abundant in some years, there are still plenty of viable acorns to ensure the survival of our oaks.

The sexual generation of the gall wasp **Andricus quercusramuli** induces the cotton wool gall on male oak catkins. Each gall contains up to 20 larval chambers but is completely concealed by a mass of white hairs up to 30 mm in diameter. The hairs turn brown as the gall matures in late spring and the galled catkins then fall to the ground. Adult gall wasps emerge in May and June and

the females lay their eggs in young buds, where the little egg-shaped galls of the asexual generation (*right*) develop in the autumn. These galls are green at first but turn brown before falling from the trees and yielding adults of the asexual generation in the spring. NB: the globular object above the cotton wool gall is a currant gall of *Neuroterus quercusbaccarum* (see p. 27).

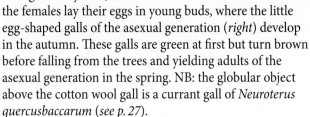

These attractive galls, up to 5 mm long, are the work of the asexual generation of the gall wasp **Andricus malpighii**. The galls are green and smooth when young in the summer and usually have a shiny white tip. Not all specimens develop the red ribs. Some also have short stalks. The galls become brown and woody as they mature in the autumn. Mature galls usually fall from the trees and the adult insects emerge in the spring to lay their eggs in the opening buds. Galls of the sexual generation develop on the male catkins and, being only 1·5 mm long, they are rarely seen.

The asexual galls of **Andricus callidoma** (*inset*) mature in May or June and are usually stalked, but otherwise they resemble those of *A. malpighii*.

The asexual galls of the gall wasp **Andricus seminationis** develop on the male catkins, which become stout and remain on the trees until well into the autumn. The galls are slightly downy and up to 14 mm long including the stalk, although galls that harbour inquilines (*see p. 12*) are often stunted and stalkless and then resemble the galls of *A. malpighii*. Mature galls fall in the autumn and adult insects emerge in the spring. No sexual generation is known.

The gall wasp **Aphelonyx cerricola** is responsible for this gall on Turkey oak twigs. Green and velvety when it first appears in the summer (*near right*), it gradually turns brown and woody. Galls are up to about 20 mm across and partially wrapped around

the twigs, but they are very irregular in shape and neighbouring galls often fuse together. Each gall has a large central chamber enclosing a small egg-shaped inner gall which contains a single larva. Pupation takes place in the galls and new adults emerge early in the spring. Only the asexual generation of the species is known at present. The galls were unknown in Britain until 1997 but now occur in many parts of England.

One of the most familiar galls, the oak apple is induced by the larvae of the sexual generation of the gall wasp **Biorhiza pallida**. Soft and spongy, it bursts from a bud in late spring and grows to a diameter of about 4 cm. Each gall contains numerous chambers, each enclosing a *Biorhiza* larva. The larvae pupate in the galls and winged adults chew their way out

in the summer, with each gall yielding either males or females. After mating, the females crawl into the ground to lay their eggs in the oak's slender rootlets. When the resulting larvae start to feed they become surrounded by spherical galls (*inset*), in which they feed for about 18 months. Adults of the asexual generation emerge at the end of the second winter. These are all wingless females and they are unaffected by the cold. They can climb the oak trunks and lay their eggs in the buds even in sub-zero temperatures. The insect's two-year life cycle means that two separate populations may exist on any one tree.

The striped pea gall of the asexual generation of the gall wasp *Cynips longiventris* is one of the most colourful of the galls on oak leaves. While the form of the gall is consistent and unmistakable, with lines of bumps blending into small ridges running across the surface, the colours are variable: red, pink, yellow, and green all feature on different examples. The galls appear on the undersides of the leaves soon after midsummer and may reach 10 mm in diameter. By early autumn, the colours fade and the galls begin to shrivel. They usually fall with the leaves and the adult wasps

emerge in the winter to lay their eggs in the dormant oak buds, where the sexual generation develops in tiny, greenish grey, hairy egg-shaped galls.

The cherry gall is induced by the asexual generation of the gall wasp *Cynips quercusfolii*. Between 15 and 25 mm in diameter when mature, it can be seen on the under-sides of the oak leaves in late summer and autumn. Single galls are common, but six or more of varying sizes may be found on one leaf. The surface is smooth when on English or pedunculate oak (*Quercus robur*) and somewhat warty when on sessile oak (*Q. petraea*). Galls on hybrids between these two oaks run between the two basic forms. Starting off pale yellowish green, the surface begins to

show a faint pink and then darkens to an ever deeper red. Just before leaf-fall the gall becomes brown and begins to wither. Usually falling with the leaves, it matures on the ground and the adult wasps emerge between late autumn and early spring. They lay their eggs in the dormant oak buds and the sexual generation develops there in little purple, egg-shaped galls. Adults of the sexual generation emerge in late spring and lay their eggs in the new leaves.

The aptly named pea gall is induced by the asexual generation of the gall wasp *Cynips divisa*. Found in late summer on the undersides of oak leaves, the smooth galls are slightly flattened and very hard. They vary in colour from yellow, through pink to red and then brown. The galls fall in the autumn and adults emerge in the winter to lay their eggs in dormant buds. Galls of the sexual generation are tiny egg-shaped or cylindrical objects, springing from the buds or attached to the edges of the young leaves in the spring. The asexual galls of *Cynips agama* are very similar to those of *C. divisa* but have very thin walls and are easily squashed.

The silk button spangle gall, caused by the asexual generation of the gall wasp *Neuroterus numismalis*, is a truly spectacular gall, especially when looked at closely. The raised edge of the cup appears to have been embroidered with silky golden hairs. Developing on the undersides of the leaves, the galls are often abundant in late summer. Hundreds may occur on a single leaf. Up to 5 mm across, each gall contains a single larva. The galls mature on the ground in the autumn and the adult wasps emerge in the spring. Eggs are laid in the oak buds and the resulting larvae induce the formation of the ….

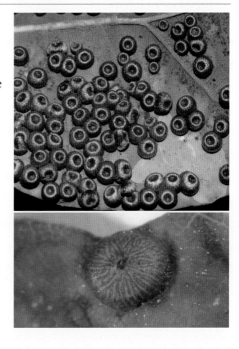

…. galls of the sexual generation on the young leaves. These galls are far harder to spot than the showy silk buttons, being small, roughly circular blisters that match the colour of the oak leaves. The barely raised dome on the upper surface is matched by a similar bulge below. The upper surface has a central pimple, from which radiating lines stretch almost to the edge. A single larva lives and pupates in each gall and the adult insects emerge from May to July.

This gall, resembling a tiny sea anemone, develops on the fertilised female flowers (incipient acorns) of Turkey oak and is caused by the sexual generation of the gall wasp **Neuroterus saliens**. Each gall contains several larvae and the adult insects emerge during the summer. Mated females then lay their eggs in the Turkey oak leaves, leading to the development of the asexual galls pictured below. The insect has been known in Britain only since 2004 but is now well established over much of southern England.

Asexual galls of the gall wasp **Neuroterus saliens** develop on the Turkey oak in the autumn, sometimes on the young shoots but normally on the mid-ribs or the petioles of the leaves – usually, but not always, on the lower surface. The spindle-shaped galls are 3–4 mm long and each contains a single larva.

Lemon yellow at first, they often become red later. Mature galls fall to the ground and the adult insects emerge in the spring to lay their eggs in the opening flowers.

Tiny egg-shaped or spherical galls on the lower sides of the veins of oak leaves are caused by the asexual generation of the gall wasp **Neuroterus anthracinus**. No more than 3 mm long, the galls are easily identified by a small flap of tissue protruding from each side of the base. Pale green or cream at first, they

usually develop reddish brown spots before maturing and falling from the leaves in the autumn. Adult insects emerge in winter and early spring to lay their eggs in buds. Galls of the sexual generation develop inconspicuously in buds among developing leaves.

Common spangle galls (*above left*) house the larvae of the asexual generation of the gall wasp **Neuroterus quercusbaccarum**. Each gall is up to 5 mm across, with a central 'pimple' and scattered tufts of red hairs. Each contains a single larva and there may be scores of galls on the underside of a single leaf. Most galls are yellow, but some are red and small numbers occasionally develop on the uppersides of the leaves. The galls fall from the leaves and pass the winter in the leaf litter, often swelling noticeably as the insects mature inside them. Adult gall wasps emerge early in the spring and lay their eggs in the oak buds. Galls of the sexual generation (*above right*) develop on the male catkins or on the young leaves and mature in late spring and early summer. Commonly known as currant galls, they are about 6 mm across, soft and juicy, and green with a variable amount of red blushing. The adult insects emerge during the summer and mated females lay their eggs in the leaves to start the cycle again.

These hairy spheres, some 5 mm in diameter (*above left*), are the galls of the sexual generation of the gall wasp **Neuroterus tricolor**. They are pale green or yellow with a variable pink tinge and the hairs range from silvery white to pink or purple. They develop on the undersides of oak leaves in the spring and neighbouring galls often coalesce. They are most often found close to the ground on saplings, but they are not common. Adult insects emerge in the summer and the females lay their eggs in the oak leaves, leading to the development of the ….

…. galls of the asexual generation of **Neuroterus tricolor** (*above right*), sometimes known as cupped spangle galls. Appearing slightly later than the other spangles, these are the only spangles occurring on lammas leaves. Up to 5 mm across, they differ from common spangle galls (*p. 27*) in having a raised rim and a more fleshy texture. The galls mature and fall from the leaves in the autumn and the adult gall wasps emerge in late spring to lay their eggs in the young oak leaves.

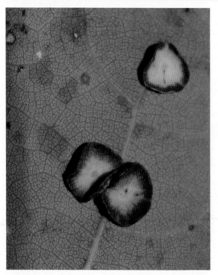

The asexual generation of the gall wasp **Neuroterus albipes** is responsible for these smooth spangle galls on the undersides of oak leaves. Up to 5 mm across, the galls are hairless and generally cream or pale green, and do not always have the pink rim shown here. The galls are noticeably thinner than the cupped spangle galls pictured above and, unlike the common spangle galls, they have a slightly raised rim. Mature galls fall from the leaves in the autumn and adult insects emerge in early spring. Galls of the sexual generation are tiny, egg-shaped objects, usually nestling between the leaf lobes in the spring.

The sexual generation of the gall wasp *Neuroterus politus* galls oak buds in spring. The egg-shaped gall is up to 12 mm long but, being green, it is not easy to spot among the opening leaves. It is our only succulent bud gall. Each gall contains a single larva, which pupates in the gall. The adult gall wasp emerges in April or May through a small hole, clearly seen in the left-hand gall. The asexual generation develops

on the male catkins, in egg-shaped galls less than 2 mm long, with adult insects emerging during the summer and laying their eggs in dormant buds.

These waxy pink galls each house a larva of the sexual generation of the gall wasp *Trigonaspis megaptera*. Up to 10 mm across and sometimes known as pink bud galls, they develop in the spring and can be found on small saplings, as pictured here, or sprouting from dormant buds on the trunks of more mature trees. Adult insects emerge in spring and early summer and mated females lay their eggs in the leaves. Larvae hatching from these eggs induce the formation of ....

.... kidney galls, which are the asexual galls of *Trigonaspis megaptera*. Often clustered along the underside of a major vein, these galls are commonly distorted and do not always exhibit the characteristic kidney shape. Mature galls, up to 4 mm long, are green or yellow. They fall from the leaves in the autumn and wingless adult insects emerge in the winter to lay their eggs in the dormant buds and produce the next sexual generation.

Macrodiplosis pustularis is one of two common gall midges that affect oak leaves. It causes the tips of the lobes to turn down and become tightly pressed to the underside of the leaf, forming flat pouches each containing a single white larva. The folded portion of the leaf loses much of its natural colour and is often heavily mottled with yellow. A similar discoloration can be seen on a slight bulge on the upper leaf surface. The gall eventually turns brown, before the rest of the leaf. The galls are common from June until the autumn, when they open slightly, allowing the larvae to fall to the ground, where they overwinter before pupating in the spring.

The gall midge *Macrodiplosis roboris* usually attacks the oak leaves between the lobes, causing the margin to fold or roll upwards. Each narrow fold contains one or more orange larvae. There is variation in the amount of natural colour retained by the galls, with many staying green and inconspicuous while others become quite pale. The degree of fleshiness also varies a good deal. The galls can be found from June until September, when they turn brown and open to allow the larvae to escape. The larvae fall to the ground and overwinter in the soil or leaf litter. Pupation occurs in the spring or early summer, when a new generation of adults emerges.

The gall mite *Acalitus brevitarsus* induces pale, slightly domed, blister-like swellings on the uppersides of alder leaves (*far right*). Below these swellings, on the underside (*near right*) of the leaf, there is a pale erineum which, when viewed with a hand lens, can be seen to consist of a mat of shiny, glass-like hairs. The mites live among and feed on the hairs. Blisters and erinea

all gradually change to rusty brown as they mature in late summer and autumn, when the mites leave to spend the winter in old cones and bark crevices.

The gall mite *Aceria nalepai* induces distinctive galls in the angles between the mid-rib and the main veins of alder leaves. The galls are arranged alternately or in pairs, starting close to the leaf stalk but not reaching the tip of the leaf. Each gall is a pouch, up to 3 mm high, with a wide, hairy opening on the underside of the leaf. Each is filled with russet hairs, among which live numerous mites. The galls are yellowish when they first appear in the spring, but become brown as they mature in late summer. The mites then leave and spend the winter in old cones and bark crevices.

These small, pimple-like galls are the work of the gall mite *Eriophyes laevis*. Up to 2 mm in diameter and more or less spherical in shape, they each have a narrow opening on the underside of the leaf. The galls may cover almost the whole upper surface of alder leaves, and such heavy infestations restrict the growth of the leaves. The galls are green in their early stages but usually become red or purple later in the year. The mites leave the galls in the autumn and spend the winter in empty cones and bark crevices. Individual leaves are occasionally affected by both *E. laevis* and *Aceria nalepai*.

The ascomycete fungus *Taphrina alni* infects the scales of female alder catkins, causing them to develop into remarkable tongue-like growths up to 20 mm long. There may be more than one growth on each catkin. They are pale cream at first, but become red or purple later. Spores are scattered from a mat of asci that covers the galls in late summer. Once regarded as quite rare, and mainly western in distribution, *T. alni* is now more widely distributed in the United Kingdom, although it still appears to be absent from the south-east.

Taphrina tosquinetii is an ascomycete fungus that distorts alder leaves by causing large blisters on both surfaces. In the early stages the edge of a leaf may simply be incurved, but later the whole leaf may become thickened and brittle, and twice as large as normal. Galled leaves are also much paler than the normal foliage. The blisters become covered with white bloom as the spore-bearing asci develop on the surface. The galls are especially common on sucker shoots in the summer.

Apple leaves commonly develop irregular, rust-like erinea on the undersides in the summer. Although sometimes mistaken for fungal infections, these are caused by various gall mites, the commonest of which is the **apple leaf mite** (*Phyllocoptes malinus*). The erinea consist of minute woolly or globular hairs amongst which the mites live and feed. Badly affected leaves may fall in late summer, but the mites have no serious effect on the trees The mites pass the winter in a dormant state under loose bark or in the buds. Eating apples and crab apples seem to suffer more than cooking varieties, although Bramleys sometimes carry heavy infestations.

Red- or purple-veined rolls on ash leaves indicate the presence of the very common psyllid *Psyllopsis fraxini*. The galls develop early in the summer, when nymphs hatching from over-wintered eggs start to feed on the leaves. Affected areas become swollen and roll downwards to form pouches that enclose the wax-covered nymphs. Two or three generations may develop in each gall, and by the end of the summer the galls may contain insects of all stages. Adult psyllids leave the galls before leaf-fall and lay their eggs on the dormant buds.

These irregular, rusty-looking lumps on the ash keys are clusters of galls caused by the gall mite *Aceria fraxinivora*, which usually attacks the flower clusters soon after they open. Individual galls are no more than 2 cm across but when massed together, as they often are, they can be very impressive. They are green at first, but soon become brown. They tend to stay on the trees through the winter, long after the unaffected keys have flown, becoming black and showing up as conspicuous silhouettes on the bare twigs. The mites pass the winter in the old galls or in bark crevices. Galls also occur, less often, on twigs and leaves.

These ash leaflets have been galled by the gall midge *Dasineura fraxini*. Most of the gall is on the underside of the main vein, where it forms a narrow green pouch containing one or more orange larvae. That part of the gall visible on the upperside of the leaflet is little more than a raised slit, although it remains closed until the larvae are ready to leave in the autumn. The larvae pupate in the soil and new adults emerge in the spring. Individual galls along the vein frequently coalesce into a single swelling. Galls can also be found on the leaf stalks and on the main axis of the leaf.

The gall-midge *Dasineura acrophila* causes young ash leaflets to fold upwards from the midrib to form a gall shaped rather like a pea-pod. The gall may be somewhat paler than the rest of the leaf and may contain 20 or more white, legless larvae. These larvae feed in the gall until they are fully grown in the middle of the summer, and then they leave and fall to the ground. They pupate in the soil and new adult midges emerge when the new ash leaves begin to open in the spring.

The psyllid *Lauritrioza alacris* galls bay leaves, causing the edges to swell and curl downwards, forming pale, elongated pouches that house one or two generations of psyllids during the summer. The pale green nymphs, covered with white wax, are easily seen by unrolling the galls. Stripy brown, winged adults (*see p. 9*) go into hibernation in the autumn, sometimes tucked up in the old galls, which have usually turned brown by this time, but more often in the leaf litter below the bushes.

These stunted, heavily pleated beech leaves have been invaded by the gall mite *Acalitus plicans*. The affected region, which may be almost the whole leaf blade or just the apical part, is covered with hairs which may be reddish in colour. The reddish tinge resembles that of the emerging leaf. This, together with the small size of the blade, makes the gall easy to overlook. The mites live and feed among the hairs, deep in the folds of the leaf. They spend the winter under the bud scales.

The gall mite *Acalitus stenaspis* galls the edges of beech leaves, causing the edges to curl upwards and form very tight rolls. These galls are so slender that they are often difficult to spot, although they sometimes stretch all the way around the leaf. Their presence can be detected by gently pressing the leaf between finger and thumb. Numerous mites live inside the rolls during the summer, feeding on a mass of extremely tiny hairs. They leave the galls before leaf-fall and spend the winter in the dormant buds.

The gall mite *Aceria nervisequa* is responsible for these felt-like galls (erinea) between the veins on the undersides of beech leaves. The same species also induces small erinea along the veins on the upper surfaces. On normal beech leaves both types of erinea are white at first, turning pinkish and then brown as summer turns to autumn, but galls on copper beech are pink from the start. A good way to detect the erinea on the lower surface is to stand under a branch and look upwards and outwards. In common with most species living on deciduous trees, the mites pass the winter in the buds or in bark crevices.

The gall midge *Hartigiola annulipes* is responsible for these cylindrical growths on beech leaves. Each gall starts out as a tiny, flattened dome, visible on both leaf surfaces in the spring and the upper part gradually lengthens into its columnar shape. Yellowish green at first, the galls often become reddish brown later, with a variable amount of hair. Not all develop pointed tips. Up to 5 mm high when mature in late summer, each gall contains a single white larva. The complete gall falls when the larva is mature, leaving a small circular hole in the leaf. Pupation takes place in the fallen galls and adult midges emerge in the following spring to lay their eggs in the young leaves.

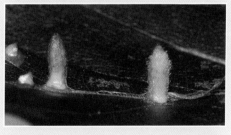

Witches' brooms, seen here looking like birds' nests on a pair of birch trees, are dense bunches of stunted twigs. These galls occur on a variety of trees, but perhaps most often on birch and hornbeam and also on gean or wild cherry. Although caused by various organisms, the most common causer of witches' brooms on birch is the ascomycete fungus *Taphrina betulina*. The galls start off as densely packed clusters of buds and sometimes resemble hedgehogs clinging to the trunks. They may remain as buds for several years and then, possibly when the fungus loses its vigour, the buds grow into scores of slender shoots. Small leaves, on which the asci develop in the spring, sprout from these twigs, but usually fall before the leaves elsewhere on the trees. Some brooms have been known to exceed one metre in diameter.

The gall mite *Acalitus calycophthirus* is responsible for 'big-bud' galls on birch twigs. Very similar to the more familiar big bud galls on black currant (*see p. 40*) and hazel (*see p. 46*), the galls consist of clustered and swollen leaves that shelter large populations of mites. The galls are silvery green when they first appear in the spring, but gradually turn brown and become quite woody. The mites remain in the galls for much of the year, passing the winter there in a dormant state and emerging to invade new buds in the following spring and early summer.

The gall midge **Massalongia ruber** induces elongated swellings in the mid-ribs of mature birch leaves. Most obvious on the undersides of the leaves, the galls often extend into the bases of the side veins, and sometimes occur on the petiole as well. They are green at first, but become purplish or brown as they  age. Each contains a single red larva, although neighbouring galls may join together. Mature larvae leave the galls in late summer to hibernate and pupate in the soil, with new adults emerging in the following spring or summer.

Small, pale, cabbage-like leaf clusters at the tips of box shoots are caused by the psyllid **Psylla buxi**. The bunched leaves are strongly concave and slightly thicker than normal leaves and during the summer they conceal numerous pale green nymphs, all coated with white wax. The insects mature and leave the galls in late summer and lay overwintering eggs in the shoots and leaves. Single leaves away from the shoot tips are commonly affected by this insect, which causes deep depressions on one side of the leaf  – usually the upper side – with corresponding bulges on the other side.

The gall wasp **Diastrophus rubi** attacks fresh green bramble stems in spring and sometimes attacks raspberry canes. Affected stems become swollen and often curved, and may have few prickles. The swellings, up to 15 cm long and about 1 cm wide, have a bumpy surface, with each bump indicating the chamber of a gall wasp larva. Both prostrate and upright stems may be attacked but the galls generally occur low down and may be hidden by other vegetation. During the summer, the galls pass from greenish yellow, through pink and purple to light brown. Each one may contain up to 200 spherical chambers, each containing a white larva. The larvae overwinter in the gall and adults emerge in the following spring. Old galls (*inset*) are often silvery and show numerous exit  holes. They may remain on the plants for years and are most noticeable during the winter months when the brambles have lost much of their foliage. The galls are most common in the south and east of Britain.

The gall midge *Lasioptera rubi* lays clusters of up to 40 eggs in young bramble shoots in early summer. Rapid proliferation of the inner tissues then produces a swelling up to 50 mm long and 25 mm across. The lumpy, rough-looking gall usually develops only on one side of the shoot, but occasionally spreads to both sides. The surface frequently bears longitudinal fissures. The gall matures in early autumn, by which time it has usually turned from green to reddish brown. It contains several irregular chambers, each lined with a fungal mycelium on which the enclosed larvae feed. The reddish larvae overwinter in the galls and pupate there in the spring, with new adults emerging in May. There is just one generation per year. *Lasioptera rubi* attacks both wild and cultivated blackberries and can also cause problems on raspberries.

Contorted bramble leaves are often a sign that the gall midge *Dasineura plicatrix* has been at work. The leaves become crumpled and pleated in spring and early summer and the veins also become swollen, often with conspicuous blackening of the adjacent tissues. The white midge larvae can be found in the folds of the leaves until early summer, when they fall out and pupate in the soil. There is just one generation each year. Although the gall is common, it is easily overlooked as just a crumpled leaf. The midge attacks raspberries as well as brambles.

The gall midge *Asphondylia sarothamni* galls both the leaf-buds and the seed pods of broom. The bud gall develops in the spring as an oval green swelling, usually stalkless but with a pointed tip. Up to 10 mm long, it contains a single midge larva. Pupation takes place in the gall, with adult midges emerging in late spring and heading for the opening flowers. The picture shows an empty pupal case protruding from the upper gall. Eggs are laid in the flowers and the resulting larvae induce galls in the walls of the pods – usually one or two to each pod and generally near the stalk. Each gall is an oval swelling about 10 mm long and, like those of the spring generation, each contains a single orange larva. New adults emerge from the pods in late summer and lay their eggs in the leaf buds, although the eggs do not hatch until the spring. Both types of gall are examples of 'ambrosia galls', in which there appears to be a close relationship between an insect causer and a fungus, although here the fungus does not provide the gall-causer with food. Once the larva stops feeding, the fungus fills the cavity and destroys the gall structure.

The gall midge **Asphondylia pilosa** also induces bud galls on broom. These galls contain fungi like those of *A. sarothamni*, but that is where the similarity ends. The *pilosa* gall is clothed with long hairs and has a long 'neck' accounting for more than half of its 10 mm length, and the species is single-brooded with no galling of the seed pods. Pupation takes place in the galls, which remain on the plants throughout the winter.

The gall mite **Aceria genistae** is responsible for these irregular grey or purplish clusters that sprout from broom buds in the spring. Up to 40 mm across, each cluster consists of numerous stunted and distorted leaves, all clothed with hairs that conceal and nourish the mites. The mites remain in the galls during the winter and move to new buds in the spring. Old galls may remain on the bushes for several years.

Pale pouches on the edges of purging buckthorn leaves are caused by the psyllid **Trichochermes walkeri**. Overwintered eggs hatch as the buds open in early spring and the nymphs start to feed on the edges of the leaves, causing adjacent areas of the margin to swell and roll up to form pouches. These are usually 5–10 mm long and there may be several on a single leaf. Each gall may contain several nymphs. Adult psyllids leave the galls in July and August and feed on sap from the leaves and twigs. They lay their eggs on the twigs and are easily mistaken for buds when sitting there.

The leaves of buckthorn and alder buckthorn are commonly galled by the rust fungus **Puccinia coronata**, which causes yellow swellings and marked distortion of leaves, petioles, and flower stalks. The swellings bear orange frilly-edged, cup-shaped or star-like aecia (*see p. 7*), which carry the aeciospores. The latter are scattered by wind or by visiting insects and germinate into new fungal threads when they reach various grasses, on which other stages of the life cycle develop.

These domed blisters on currant leaves are the galls of the aphid *Cryptomyzus ribis*. They occur mainly on red and white currants, although black currants are not immune to attack. The blisters are yellow when they first appear, soon after the leaves open in spring, but usually turn red as they mature in early summer. The leaves often become crinkled and the yellowish green aphids cluster in hairy depressions on the underside. Mature aphids leave the galls and fly to hedge woundwort plants, where they produce several more generations. In the autumn the aphids return to the currant bushes and lay their overwintering eggs on the twigs.

Big-bud galls of black currant are caused by the gall mite *Cecidophyopsis ribis*. Infested buds swell up and may reach 10 mm in diameter, but they do not open. They are more rounded than normal buds and contain huge numbers of mites. The latter live in the galls for much of the year and emerge just as the flowers start to open. Wafted by the breeze or carried by visiting insects, the lucky ones reach new buds where they settle down and breed. As well as causing direct damage to the host plants, the mites carry reversion disease, a viral infection that affects leaves and flowers and can lead to a marked reduction in fruit yield.

This attractive gall, commonly known as a rivet gall, develops on dogwood leaves in response to the presence of larvae of the gall midge *Craneiobia corni*. It is greenish yellow at first, but becomes red or purple as it matures. It resembles a small up-turned bottle, with a rounded base up to 5 mm across on the upper surface of the leaf and a tubular neck up to 10 mm long protruding from the lower surface. The galls normally occur

in small clusters. Each one contains one or more thick-walled cavities and each cavity contains an orange larva. Mature larvae leave the galls in late summer and overwinter in the soil before pupating and producing new adults in the spring. Rivet galls are most common in southern England.

The gall mite **Epitrimerus trilobus** is responsible for the roll galls that are common on the leaves of elder during the spring and summer. The leaf margins roll upwards, the rolls being up to 5 mm wide and often extending all around the leaf. Young leaves may become severely crumpled and fail to open properly, as pictured below. The mites leave the galls in late summer and spend the next few months in a dormant state in the buds or bark crevices.

The gall midge **Placochela nigripes** infests the flower buds of elder and prevents them from opening. The swollen petals form a cap, which conceals an orange larva. The cap may remain green, but frequently turns pink or purple as shown here. The two green globules are ripening fruits, unaffected by the midge. The galls mature in late summer, when the larvae escape to spend the winter in the soil prior to pupation in the spring. This gall midge attacks privet buds in the same way and the swollen white buds can be found on both wild and cultivated species.

41

Smooth pouches up to 15 mm high on elm leaves are caused by the aphid *Tetraneura ulmi* and are commonly known as fig galls. Half a dozen or more galls may develop on a single leaf. They vary in shape and several aphids grow up in each gall in early summer. Mature insects – all asexual females – leave through one or more openings in the gall wall and fly away to breed on grass roots in the summer. Winged forms return to the elms in the autumn and give birth to tiny wingless males and females. After mating, each female lays just one egg, from which an asexual female nymph hatches in the spring. Each nymph starts to feed on the underside of a leaf, which reacts by forming a tiny yellowish pimple on the upper side – the beginning of the gall, into which the young aphid soon moves to feed and produce her offspring.

The gall mite *Aceria campestricola* is the cause of these pimples on elm leaves. Hundreds of galls may occur on a single leaf. Up to 1 mm across, they are rounded above and each has a small conical projection on the lower leaf surface. They are often greenish yellow, but tend to redden when exposed to the sun. The mites pass the winter in bark crevices and attack the leaves as soon as they open in the spring. Although abundant on English elm and other small-leaved species, the mite does not seem to attack wych elm.

These small turret-like galls erupting from the veins of elm leaves in late spring are caused by the larvae of the gall midge *Janetiella lemeei*. The turrets may appear on either the upper or lower surface of the leaf, with small domes on the opposite side. Up to 8 mm across, each gall contains a single yellow larva, which leaves the gall when fully grown and hibernates in the soil before pupating in the spring. The galls can be found on all kinds of elms.

This bladder-like gall, up to 8 cm across, is the work of the aphid ***Eriosoma lanuginosum***, the feeding of which causes almost the whole leaf to convert itself into the thin-walled bladder. At least the basal part is noticeably grooved or fluted. The gall contains numerous aphids. It is pale green at first, with a somewhat mealy or hairy surface, but it becomes smoother later and often takes on a red or purplish tinge. It becomes brown when the aphids mature and leave in late summer, and old galls commonly remain on the trees long after the normal leaves have fallen. Aphids leaving the galls in summer migrate to feed on the roots of pear and quince trees. Their progeny return to the elms to lay their eggs in the autumn.

The aphid ***Eriosoma ulmi*** is responsible for this common yellowish-green or pinkish gall, which develops when one half of the elm leaf blade becomes crinkled and rolls in to form a tubular pouch. The galls are most conspicuous on wych elm, which has larger leaves, and therefore larger galls, than the other elms. Numerous waxy aphids develop in the pouch in spring and early summer. Winged aphids – all females – leave the galls in June and July and fly to currant bushes, where they live and reproduce on the roots. In the autumn their progeny fly back to the elm trees, where both males and females are produced and the mated females lay overwintering eggs. The much rarer *Eriosoma grossulariae* induces similar galls, but this aphid is not waxy.

The gall midge *Asphondylia ulicis* galls gorse buds early in the spring, causing them to swell and become somewhat hairier than normal. Both flower and leaf buds are attacked, and each gall contains a pale orange-yellow larva. The gall cavity is lined with fungal mycelium, which is white at first but later becomes black in colour. The larvae mature in late spring and pupate in their galls, where the pupae remain until the following spring.

These pale patches on hawthorn leaves are the galls of the gall mite *Eriophyes crataegi*. Each is a little blister, barely raised from both leaf surfaces and containing numerous mites. The mites spend the winter in bark crevices or among the bud scales and begin their attack on the leaves as soon as the latter unfurl in the spring. Although pale at first, the affected tissues gradually turn brown. A single leaf on a tree may be the only one so affected, but sometimes every leaf is galled – with a truly startling effect.

Tight rolls on the edges of hawthorn leaves are induced by the gall mite *Phyllocoptes goniothorax*. The mites may be so prolific that almost every leaf on a tree is affected. The rolls are up to 15 mm long and average about 2 mm in diameter. The mites leave the galls in late summer and spend the winter in the buds or in bark crevices, emerging to attack the new leaves as soon as they open in the spring. An crineum on the under surface of the leaf is the rarer kind of gall induced by the same mite.

Untidy rosettes on the terminal shoots of hawthorns are the galls of the gall midge **Dasineura crataegi**. They are particularly conspicuous along the hedgerows in September, when new growth has stretched upwards and provided fresh foliage, and the silhouette allows recognition even from moving vehicles. The rosettes of earlier generations in spring and summer are less noticeable. The midge appears to favour hedgerows rather than free-standing trees. Each rosette is an irregular cluster of many thickened and distorted leaves that usually bear lots of small red or green, hair-like outgrowths. Many orange-red, legless larvae inhabit each gall. The rosettes stay on the twigs after the other foliage has fallen, but the fully-grown larvae leave to pupate in the soil. There are two or three generations each year.

Large bright red or purplish swellings taking up a significant proportion of the upper surface of tender young hawthorn leaves early in the season are due to the gall-causing aphid **Dysaphis crataegi**. The colourful blisters are matched by concavities on the under surface which contain the pale green or pinkish aphids responsible for the growths. In June the aphids migrate to spend the summer breeding on an alternate host, which may be wild or cultivated carrots or some other umbellifer. The empty galls then gradually lose their vivid hues. Pale exoskeletons of the aphids may remain inside them for some time, together with various other insects that make use of the shelter. In the autumn, some of the aphids fly back to the hawthorns, where they lay their overwintering eggs.

Abnormally swollen buds on hazel twigs are the work of the gall mite *Phytoptus avellanae*. The galls, commonly known as 'big-buds', are green, yellowish, or reddish-brown and up to 10 mm in diameter. Each may consist of 20–40 stunted leaf-scales, the inner ones being thickened and hairy, and can contain hundreds of mites. The feeding activities of the latter completely destroy the young leaves or female flowers enclosed within the scales. The galls open up in late spring, allowing the mites to leave and enter new buds.

The distorted hazel catkin pictured here has been attacked by the gall midge *Contarinia coryli,* whose jumping white larvae live between the swollen scales of the young catkins throughout the summer. The larvae fall to the ground in the autumn and pass the winter in the soil, although they do not pupate until the spring. New adults emerge in late spring and eggs are laid in the developing catkins. Very similar galls are induced by the gall mite *Phyllocoptruta coryli*, although the affected catkins tend to be less symmetrical than those attacked by the midge and the affected scales are often somewhat ragged. The two galls can be distinguished with certainty only when the mites or midge larvae are present, but it is not uncommon for the two creatures to be present in a single catkin.

Honey locust trees may be badly disfigured by the activity of the gall midge *Dasineura gleditchiae*, whose larvae cause the leaflets to curl up and form brown pod-like galls. The larvae range from white to orange and there may be several generations in a year. Larvae of the summer generations pupate in the galls while those maturing in the autumn fall with the leaves and then burrow into the soil. They pupate in the spring and the new adults soon emerge to lay their eggs on the new leaflets and start the cycle again. *D. gleditchiae* is an American insect only recently established in Europe.

The gall midge *Zygiobia carpini* galls the veins of hornbeam leaves, usually attacking the edges of the mid-rib on the underside of the leaf (*near right*) and producing a row of pale swellings up to 4 mm across. These frequently develop in the angles of the veins and they often form double rows. Their position is marked by a slight crumpling of the upper surface as well (*far right*). Each gall contains a single white larva, which leaves

its home and falls to the ground in the autumn, passing the winter in the soil before pupating in the spring and producing a new adult in late spring or early summer.

The gall mite *Aceria tenella* induces shiny brown pimples on the upper surfaces of hornbeam leaves. The galls develop in the angles between the mid-rib and the other veins, and each has a hairy opening on the underside of the leaf. The maximum diameter is about 5 mm. The mites leave in the autumn and, in common with most other gall mites associated with trees and shrubs, they spend the winter in a dormant state, tucked up in bark crevices and other small spaces.

The gall midge *Contarinia tiliarum* usually induces globular galls on the petioles or mid-ribs of lime leaves. Less often, the galls can be found on young shoots, on the flower stalks, or in the fruit bracts. Depending on the site, the gall is between 4 and 15 mm in diameter. It is usually quite pale, although some examples are deep green or take on a reddish tinge. Each gall contains a number of chambers, each containing a single lemon-yellow larva that wriggles dramatically when exposed. Mature larvae leave the galls in autumn and pass the winter in the soil.

These 'pimples' are caused by the gall midge *Didymomyia tiliacea* and affect both surfaces of the leaf. Young galls are conical above and rounded on the lower leaf surface. In the middle of the summer a woody, cylindrical or egg-shaped inner gall develops and protrudes from the cone rather like an egg sitting in an egg-cup. Each is occupied by a single yellow

larva. Later in the summer the inner gall separates and falls to the ground, leaving a circular crater as pictured here. The larva pupates inside the fallen gall and a new adult emerges in the following spring. If the gall falls early enough the crater may be filled in, but there is usually no doubt that the leaf has been galled by this midge.

The gall midge *Dasineura thomasiana* causes young terminal lime leaves to become rolled or crumpled and abnormally hairy. The veins are distinctly thickened. The resulting gall encloses a number of midge larvae, which are white at first but become orange or pale red as they grow. The optimum time to find the larvae is early June, before they leave the galls to pupate in the soil. In some seasons and in some areas there may be a second generation of galls in late July, but otherwise the pupae remain in the soil until the following spring.

These pale patches are the galls of the gall mite *Eriophyes leiosoma*. Each gall is usually a little over 5 mm in diameter and usually forms a slight bulge, although it is sometimes simply a yellowish patch. The 'working part' of the gall is on the underside of the leaf, in the form of an erineum composed of a mass of short hairs with rounded tips. The mite *Phytoptus erinotes* induces a much more distinct upward bulge, a trifle less in diameter, and its erineum hairs are slender and pointed.

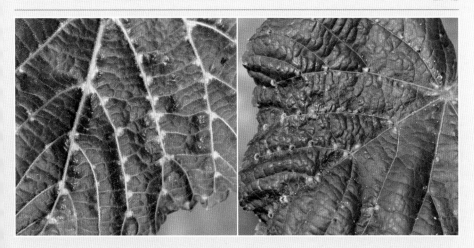

Galls induced by the gall mite **Eriophyes exilis** appear on lime leaves from May onwards. The galls are no more than 2 to 3 mm in height, but their form and position are distinctive. Each is a regular hemispherical greenish-yellow to brown pimple (*above right*) covered in short hairs, sitting tightly in the angle between two veins. When large numbers of galls are present the regular pattern is very conspicuous, and it is unique to lime leaf galls. The concavity below each gall on the underside of the leaf is surrounded by a raised edge which is also covered by short hairs (*above left*). The hairs on both surfaces are white at first, but gradually become brown.

Several organisms induce roll galls on the edges of lime leaves. Some cause the edges to roll upwards and others induce downward rolls, and the rolls also vary a good deal in thickness. Those pictured here are the galls of the gall mite *Phytoptus tetratrichus*, in which the leaf margin curls downwards to form a roll 1–2 mm in diameter. Both surfaces of the gall are clothed with short hairs. Although individual galls may be quite short, they commonly join up and affect the whole leaf margin. The rolls are green to start with but often become reddish brown later. This mite can also induce erinea on the leaves of some lime species.

These brightly coloured galls, induced by the gall mite *Eriophyes tiliae*, are commonly known as nail galls and they often occur in huge numbers on the leaves of large-leaved lime and the hybrid common lime from June onwards, mainly on the lower branches. Usually between 8 and 15 mm in height, each gall tapers to a fairly sharp point. It is full of tiny, pale hairs among which the mites feed. A hole fringed with short pale hairs on the underside of the leaf allows the mites to escape in the autumn. Winter is passed in bark crevices, especially around the bases of the buds, from where the mites can easily make their way to the young leaves in the spring.

Nail galls on the leaves of the small-leaved lime are induced by the gall mite *Eriophyes lateannulatus*. These nails are shorter than those of *E. tiliae*, being no more than 5 mm in height, and are blunt at the tip. The appearance is distinctly stubby rather than tapering. The gall opening on the under side of the leaf is surrounded by a fringe of tiny hairs. The mites live in the 'nail', crawling between the masses of tubular hairs on which they feed. Pale at first, the galls soon change to a distinctive orange-red that remains throughout the summer. There may be hundreds of them on a single leaf. The mites leave the galls before leaf-fall and spend the winter in bark crevices. In common with *E. tiliae*, this mite also galls the common lime – a hybrid between the large-leaved and small-leaved limes – which is abundant in parks and city streets.

This felt gall or erineum of field maple is caused by the gall mite *Aceria eriobia* and can be found from mid-summer onwards. The erineum, composed of dense hairs, shelters numerous mites. White or cream at first, it gradually becomes red and then brown. It may cover the whole lower leaf surface and cause folding, as pictured here, with or without a bulge on the upper leaf surface. The mites leave the galls before leaf-fall and spend the winter in bark crevices.

The gall mite *Aceria myriadeum* causes these bright red pustules on field maple. The rounded pustules are 1–3 mm high and each contains several mites. There may be hundreds of galls on a single leaf. Greenish yellow at first, they mature in late summer. The mites escape through tiny, hair-fringed holes on the underside before leaf-fall and pass the winter in bark crevices. Similar galls on sycamore are caused by *Aceria cephaloneus*.

51

These volcano-like galls, up to 6 mm high on sycamore, are caused by the gall mite *Aceria macrorhyncha*, although the shape is not always as regular as that pictured here. Hairy openings on the lower leaf surface lead into the mite-filled galls. In common with other mites galling sycamore and maples, the adults overwinter in crevices on twigs and branches and emerge to lay eggs on the new leaves in spring.

These hard, rounded pustules on field maple leaves are the galls of the gall mite *Aceria macrochela*. They normally form close to the veins and have a diameter of 2–4 mm. There are rarely more than a few dozen on each leaf. They are green at first, and those developing in the shade may remain green throughout the summer. Adult mites escape through pores on the lower leaf surface in the autumn and overwinter on the twigs. Similar galls on silver maple are caused by the mite *Vasates quadripedes*.

These felt galls on sycamore leaves are caused by the gall mite ***Aceria pseudoplatani***. The erineum, on the lower surface of the leaf, feeds and shelters the mites. Cream or white at first (or pink on purple-leaved forms), it turns brown later. Its position is usually marked on the upper surface of the leaf by a distinct bulge, which is yellowish at first and then brown and dry. The mites leave the erinea in the autumn and overwinter on the twigs and branches. The black spots on the upper surface of the leaf are caused by tar spot fungus – not a gall.

The fungus **Gymnosporangium sabinae**, commonly known as the European pear rust, is responsible for these barnacle-like growths on the underside of pear leaves. Each gall is accompanied by a conspicuous yellow patch on both leaf surfaces. Spores released from the outer, brush-like part of the gall invade the stems of the introduced *Juniperus sabina*, where the complex life cycle is completed. The rust occurs on wild pear and on many cultivars and has become much more frequent in recent years.

The gall mite **Eriophyes pyri**, commonly known as the pear leaf blister mite, causes blisters to develop on pear leaves and also on young fruits. The adult mites overwinter in the buds and feed on the undersides of the young leaves in the spring, causing blister-like galls to appear on both leaf surfaces. Eggs are laid in the blisters and the mites feed there. Two or three generations may be produced during the summer months. The blisters are greenish yellow at first, but gradually turn pink or red and eventually brown or black. The same mite species galls rowan leaves (*see p. 62*).

These red spheres on aspen leaves are the galls of the gall midge **Harmandiola tremulae**. Up to 4 mm across, they have thick, hard walls and open through a slight protrusion on the lower side of the leaf. Each gall contains a single orange-red larva. Fully grown larvae leave the galls in late summer and pass the winter in the soil before pupating in the spring. Galls of **H. globuli** are similar but have thinner walls and each rests in a shallow cup.

These yellow bulges on poplar leaves are the galls of the ascomycete fungus **Taphrina populina**. The undersides of the leaves bear corresponding cavities lined with the bright yellow asci in which the spores are produced. Galls can be found throughout the summer on black poplar and its hybrids, especially the Lombardy poplar. Sometimes the galls are reversed, with the bulges on the lower surface and the cavities on the upper surface. Spores from the galls re-infect the new leaf buds in autumn and winter.

Saperda populnea is a beetle whose larvae live in the twigs of various poplars, especially the aspen. Eggs are laid in the twigs in the middle of the summer and the feeding activities of the larvae cause the surrounding tissues to swell and form more or less spherical or egg-shaped galls up to 25 mm long. Egg-laying females usually lay several eggs in each twig, leading to several adjacent galls some three or four centimetres apart. The young beetle feeds for about 15 months and then pupates in the gall, with the new adult emerging in the summer two years after starting life as an egg.

The gall mite **Phyllocoptes populi** galls aspen leaves, inducing erinea that are yellowish at first and bright red later. The erinea are usually on the lower surface, with a yellowish bulge above, but sometimes occur on the upper surface as well. Galls appear on the young leaves in the spring, when the mites move out from their winter quarters in the buds and bark crevices. The red swellings seen at the junction of the leaf blade and petiole are the galls of the much rarer gall mite *Eriophyes diversipunctatus*.

Rounded swellings in the petioles of aspens and, more rarely, other poplars, are the galls of the gall midge **Contarinia petioli**. Up to 8 mm across, the galls contain one or more orange larvae in the summer. The mature larvae leave the galls in late summer and overwinter in the soil, pupating there and producing new adults in the spring. Galls sometimes develop in the leaf mid-rib or in young shoots close to the leaf bases. Neighbouring galls often coalesce to form elongated swellings.

The aphid **Pemphigus bursarius** induces this pouch-like gall, 8–15 mm long and 6–8 mm wide, on poplar petioles, especially those of black poplar and the hybrid Lombardy poplar. The gall develops in spring when a wingless female aphid hatches from an egg that has survived the winter concealed in the bark and pierces the petiole of a young leaf to feed on the sap. In response, the plant cells multiply and enclose the aphid. Numerous progeny develop in the gall and winged females escape in early summer through a beak-like opening. They fly to lettuces and sowthistles, where they live on the roots for a few months before their progeny fly back to the poplars to lay their overwintering eggs.

The aphid **Pemphigus populinigrae** is responsible for this gall on poplar leaves. The gall is a pouch up to 25 mm long, green at first, but becoming yellow or red as it matures and then brown. Numerous female aphids develop in the gall in early summer and leave through a slit on the underside. They fly to cudweeds, where further generations develop before flying back to the poplars to lay their overwintering eggs.

The aphid **Pemphigus spyrothecae** induces this spiral gall on poplar petioles, especially those of black poplar and the hybrid Lombardy poplar. A female aphid hatches from an overwintered egg and her feeding activities cause the young petiole to swell and form the characteristic spiral around her. The young gall is green, but often becomes red as it matures and then turns brown. Up to 12 mm in length, it has 2–3 rings. Inside the gall, the aphid gives birth to perhaps 30 wingless females in June, and these produce a second generation a month later. The aphids of this generation have wings, and when the coils loosen in August they leave the gall to lay eggs on the twigs and bark. Unlike *P. bursarius*, this species does not use another host plant in the summer. The closely related *P. protospirae* induces similar galls, but they usually have more than three coils.

The gall midge **Asphondylia pruniperda** attacks the buds of blackthorn and other *Prunus* species, including cultivated plums, in the spring. Affected buds swell and form globular galls with a distinct beak. The galls are no more than 5 mm in diameter and thus not easy to see, although they are quite common. Green at first, often with a brown tip, they gradually turn brown all over. Each gall contains a single orange larva in a large cavity which, like those of other *Asphondylia* galls (*see p. 38*) is lined with fungus. The insects spend the winter in the galls and pupate early in the spring.

The pink pimples that commonly decorate blackthorn leaves, especially around the edges, are the galls of the gall mite **Eriophyes similis**. They can be found from late spring until the autumn. Mites escape through narrow openings, usually on the upper surface, and overwinter in bark crevices. The mite also galls the leaves of domestic plums, but here the galls tend to be green.

The gall mite **Phyllocoptes eupadi** induces these somewhat columnar and rather hairy pimples on bird cherry. The galls commonly cluster around the mid-rib and are up to 2 mm high, each with a small hairy opening on the underside of the leaf. The adult mites pass the winter under the bark and in other narrow crevices, including the spaces between the bud scales.

These deformed blackthorn fruits (sloes) have been galled by the ascomycete fungus **Taphrina pruni**. They are often called pocket plums because the fungus destroys the developing stone and seed, leaving a little pocket in each fruit. The galls are green at first, but become grey or brown as the spore-bearing asci develop on the outside. The spores infect the stems during the summer and the fungus grows there, ready to invade the next year's fruits. Cultivated plums and other related fruits, such as mirabelles, are also galled by this fungus.

The ascomycete fungus ***Taphrina padi*** galls the fruits of bird cherry, causing them to elongate and resemble small white or grey candles, although these galls are bright pink on bronze-leaved varieties of the host plant. The galls are hollow, like those of the blackthorn (*opposite*). The fungus enters the fruits from the stems, as in the blackthorn, and may also affect the leaves.

Peach leaf curl is caused by the ascomycete fungus ***Taphrina deformans***. Young leaves develop puckered yellow and red patches that later become greyish as the spore-bearing asci develop on them. Infected leaves usually fall prematurely. The fungus passes the winter in bark crevices and between bud scales, from where it readily invades the new leaves. Several aphids also cause crinkling of peach leaves, but do not cause the thick and colourful patches that characterise the gall.

These colourful galls, caused by the larvae of the gall midge **Putoniella pruni,** are essentially the swollen midribs of blackthorn leaves, but the leaves become so tightly rolled and distorted that it is often difficult to interpret the structure. The orange larvae can be found in the galls in spring and early summer, after which they escape through a slit in the upper wall and

become dormant in the soil before pupating early in the following spring. Although found mainly on blackthorn, the galls are occasionally a nuisance on cultivated plums on the continent.

These tightly-rolled rose leaflets are the galls of the sawfly **Blennocampa phyllocolpa**. Wild and cultivated roses are equally affected and the leaflets start to roll downwards as soon as the female sawfly prods them in her search for suitable egg-laying sites (*see p. 10*). The bright green larvae feed inside the rolls for about two months in late spring and early summer and then leave to spend the winter in the soil before pupating in the spring and giving rise

to tiny black adults, no more than about 4·5 mm long. Not all of the rolled leaflets actually contain eggs or larvae, for the female does not lay in every site she explores.

The gall midge **Dasineura rosae** attacks wild roses, causing the leaflets to fold up and form pod-like swellings – sometimes affecting the complete leaflet. The galls may remain green, but commonly assume a pink or red coloration. Each contains numerous larvae, which are white at first and orange when mature. Fully-grown larvae leave the galls to pupate in the soil. There are several generations in a year and occupied galls can be found from early spring until leaf-fall.

The robin's pincushion, also known as the bedeguar gall, develops on wild roses after the gall wasp *Diplolepis rosae* has laid its eggs in a bud in the spring. Growing mainly on the stem, it can reach 7 cm across, but small galls also occur on the leaves. Each gall has a woody core surrounded by tough, branched, green or red hairs. The core usually has many chambers, each occupied by a *Diplolepis* larva (*see p. 11*). The galls become brown in autumn and lose most of their hairs, but they remain on the bushes through the winter. New gall wasps emerge in the spring, just in time to lay their eggs on the opening buds. Males are very rare in this species and most females lay fertile eggs without mating. The gall is known as the 'sleep apple' in Germany, as it is said to aid sleep if placed under one's pillow.

Galls of the gall wasp *Diplolepis mayri* also develop on wild roses. Mature galls are superficially similar to bedeguar galls, but they are clothed with short, unbranched spines and the body of the gall is usually clearly visible. The more or less spherical galls often develop in clusters and commonly fuse together. Although they usually develop on the stems, they are occasionally found on the leaves and even on the fruits. Soft and green at first, they normally become red as they age and then become hard and brown, often losing their spines in the autumn. *D. mayri* has a life cycle similar to that of *D. rosae*, but it is a much rarer insect and probably confined to the southern half of England.

The gall wasp *Diplolepis nervosa* induces two kinds of galls on wild roses, usually on the undersides of the leaves but sometimes on the upper surface and occasionally on the flower stalks. The more easily identified form is the spiked pea or sputnik gall (*right*), which bears one or more stout spines. The smooth pea gall (*below*) lacks spines and is indistinguishable from the gall of the closely related *Diplolepis eglanteriae*, although the adult wasps are easily separated by their wing venation. Reliable identification of smooth pea galls thus requires the rearing of the adult wasps.

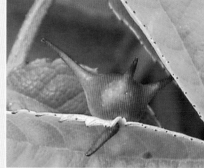

Both spiked and smooth galls develop singly or in small groups and reach about 5 mm in diameter. They vary from green, through yellow, to pink, and those on the uppersides of the leaves may become deep red in the sunlight. Each gall contains just a single gall wasp. The point of attachment is very slight and the galls are easily detached. They fall from the leaves when they mature

in the autumn, by which time they have often turned brown. The insects pupate in the galls and new adults emerge in the spring or early summer.

Galls of the gall wasp *Diplolepis spinosissimae* develop mainly on the burnet rose and are thus particularly common on coastal sites and other sandy areas, although they do sometimes occur on dog roses. Unlike the pea galls above, they protrude from both leaf surfaces and are not easily detached. They also tend to be more oval and often fuse together in small groups. Although most common on the mid-rib, they also occur on the stems and leaf stalks, and occasionally on the flowers. Stem galls remain on the host

plants through the winter, but others fall with the leaves. The life cycle of the insect resembles that of *Diplolepis nervosa*.

The gall midge *Janetiella frankumi* galls the stems of burnet rose, causing conspicuous red swellings that each contain several orange larvae. The galls are fully developed by July or August, when they split open to release the larvae. The latter then make their way into the soil, where they pass the winter in silken cocoons before pupating in the spring. Old galls remain on the host plants for some time. The galls have been known for over a century, but the gall midge itself was not described and named – as a new species – until 2003. It is a very local species and galls are found mainly in coastal areas, especially on sand dunes – the favoured habitat of the host plant – although they also occur on well-drained limestone areas.

This rowan leaf has been galled by the rust fungus **Gymnosporangium cornutum**. The yellow blobs on the underside of the leaf are the actual galls, while the brown 'horns' are the aecia of the fungus (*see p. 7*), which open at the tip to release the aeciospores. The galls are also visible as yellow swellings on the upper leaf surface. Another stage of the fungus forms galls on juniper twigs and produces the teliospores (*see p. 7*).

The gall mite **Eriophyes pyri** galls the leaves of rowan or mountain ash and various other members of the rose family, including cultivated pears (*see p. 53*). It causes domed pustules that are visible on both leaf surfaces. Green or yellow at first, the pustules later turn brown and the mites escape through pores on either surface to pass the winter in the buds or in bark crevices. The gall mite **Phyllocoptes sorbeus** also galls rowan leaves, especially in northern areas, inducing dense white, pink, or yellowish erinea on both upper and lower surfaces.

Among the commonest growths on sallow leaves, these small pouches are caused by the gall midge **Iteomyia capreae**. Up to 4 mm in diameter, the galls are hard, green domes, usually developing a reddish or purplish tinge as they mature. They open on the lower leaf surface through red-rimmed conical pores (*inset*). Each gall contains a single larva, which is white at first but then orange or red. Mature larvae drop from the galls to overwinter in the soil before pupating in the spring.

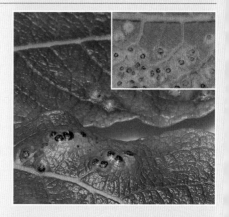

Galls of the gall midge **Iteomyia major** can be confused with those of *Iteomyia capreae* but they are larger and usually occur in fused groups of up to 10 hard, round galls. The growths are equally prominent on the lower leaf surface, where they open through circular pores that are frequently ringed with red (*right, below*). Each gall contains a single larva, resembling that of *Iteomyia capreae*, that matures in late summer and then falls to the ground to overwinter in the soil and pupate in the spring. Although these galls occur on several sallows, they are most common on *Salix cinerea*.

The gall mite *Aceria iteina* induces the formation of these small pouches on sallow leaves. Up to 4 mm high and irregularly stalked, the galls are yellowish green at first but become red as they mature. Unlike the galls of *Aculus laevis* (*below*), they are hairless on the outside, although full of hairs inside. The hairs do not protrude through the openings on the lower leaf surface. The mites escape through these pores before leaf-fall and spend the winter in the buds or in bark crevices.

Aculus laevis is the gall mite responsible for these slightly hairy and more or less spherical galls found on the sallows *Salix caprea* and *Salix cinerea* in the summer. 1–2 mm high and firmly attached to the leaves, the galls are yellowish-green at first but later turn reddish-brown. They project from the upper leaf surface and there is an elliptical opening on the underside. The interior is filled with hairs. There may  be up to 30 galls on a single leaf. The mites pass the winter in bark crevices or among the bud scales. Similar galls on willows are caused by *Aculus tetanothrix*.

The gall midge **Rabdophaga salicis** induces smooth, globular or cylindrical swellings on the shoots of various sallows and willows. The galls are usually 10–40 mm long and about 10 mm wide. There may be up to 50 chambers in a single gall, each containing a reddish larva which feeds on the pith inside the gall. The galls mature in October, the larvae over-wintering in the galls and pupating in the spring. New adults appear in May or early June.

Rabdophaga marginemtorquens is one of several gall midges responsible for the down-rolling of the edges of the leaves of various *Salix* species, although this one confines its activities to the narrow leaves of the osier. The adult midges lay their eggs between the bud scales in the spring and the resulting yellowish-red or orange larvae attack the opening leaves. The rolls, which vary in length and often run together, commonly have red, white, or orange patches. There are two or three generations in a year, with the summer generations pupating in the galls and autumn-maturing larvae pupating in the soil.

These rosette or artichoke galls on white willow are the work of the gall midge **Rabdophaga rosaria**. Each gall consists of 30 or more short, closely-packed leaves with a single pinkish midge larva in the centre. The galls mature and turn brown in late summer, but they remain on the trees throughout the winter, with the larvae or pupae still inside them. The insect galls some other *Salix* species, inducing rosettes up to 80 mm across on the broader-leaved sallows.

The sawfly **Pontania proxima** is the cause of the shiny red bean galls that develop on narrow-leaved willows. Up to 12 mm long and 6 mm wide, the galls project from both leaf surfaces and each normally contains a single larva although, because gall formation is initiated by a substance injected by the egg-laying female (*see p. 10*), some galls contain no larvae – perhaps because the eggs did not hatch or because the female did not actually deposit any eggs. There are two broods each year, with galls of the first brood maturing around mid-summer and those of the second brood in the autumn. The galls are green at first and quite hard, but they soon become red and the walls soften as the larvae consume the inner tissues. Mature larvae chew their way out of the galls, leaving just hollow shells, and pupate in yellow cocoons, either tucked into bark crevices or in the soil or leaf litter. Similar galls on sallows are caused by *Pontania bridgmanii* (*below*).

The sawfly **Pontania bridgmanii** induces bean galls on sallows. These galls resemble those of *P. proxima* (*above*) but are usually a little smaller – about 8 mm long and 4 mm wide. Unlike the *P. proxima* galls, they often develop on or close to the mid-rib, and they commonly have a narrow rim around the edge on the upper surface. They are green and hard at first, but they soon turn red and the walls soften as the larvae grow and hollow out the galls. Fully grown larvae leave their galls and pupate in the soil. There are two generations in a year and galls can be found from May until leaf-fall.

The sawfly *Eupontania pedunculi* induces globular or ovoid galls, up to 5 mm in diameter, on the undersides of sallow leaves. The gall is basically pale green or yellow, commonly bearing numerous small warts and not always tinged with red. The surface may be hairy, especially on *Salix caprea*. The gall's position is marked on the upper surface of the leaf by a yellowish scar, either flush with the surface or very slightly raised. Galls on *Salix caprea* are usually near the tip of the leaf, while on *Salix cinerea* they tend to occur more towards the middle of the leaf. The life cycle of *Eupontania pedunculi* is like that of *Pontania bridgmanii*, with two generations in a year.

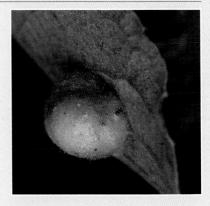

The sawfly *Eupontania viminalis* is responsible for these attractive galls on osiers and some other willows, especially the shrubby species. The galls develop on the underside of the leaf, but their positions are marked on the upper surface by circular depressions with raised brownish rims. The galls are usually hairless and young ones are often egg-shaped with conspicuously pointed apices. Each gall contains a single larva, which matures towards the end of the summer and then leaves the gall to pupate in the soil.

The gall mite *Stenacis euonymi* galls the leaf margins of spindle, causing them to curl upwards and form tight rolls. The galls, which may be green or red, often completely surround the leaf and contain large numbers of mites. They can be found from early spring until leaf-fall, by which time the mites have left to spend the winter in buds and bark crevices.

These spiky and rather waxy growths are caused by the aphid **Adelges laricis,** one of several closely related species galling spruce trees. The needle bases swell up and enclose small cavities in which the young aphids feed. When the aphids are mature, in June, the needle bases shrink and gape, allowing the aphids to escape. The aphids then fly to larch trees, where they live and breed for the next twelve months without

causing galls. Then they return to the spruce trees and spend the winter at the bases of the buds before inducing new galls in the spring. Galls of this kind are commonly known as pineapple galls.

These pineapple galls are the work of the aphid **Adelges abietis** which, unlike *Adelges laricis*, spends all its life on spruce trees and reproduces entirely by parthenogenesis: males are unknown. Gall formation begins when the females start to feed on the buds in the spring. The young nymphs then move into the incipient gall cavities and feed there until late summer. The edges of the cavities

usually become pink or red before they open. The new adults overwinter on the trees and start the cycle again in the spring. Shoot growth often continues beyond the galls of *Adelges abietis*, but not in the otherwise similar gall of *Adelges viridis*.

Galls of the aphid **Adelges cooleyi** resemble those of *A. abietis* but are usually longer and often strongly curved. They are found mainly on Sitka spruce. Young galls are pale green or yellowish and when they mature in late summer the edges of the cavities become reddish. Old galls, in common with those of other *Adelges* species, become hard and woody.

Walnut leaves are commonly galled by the gall mite *Aceria erinea*, which causes marked blistering of the upper surface. The corresponding hollows on the undersides of the leaves are lined with an erineum of white or pale brown hairs (*inset*) among which the mites live and feed. Galls are also occasionally found on the young fruits. The mites spend the winter in the buds.

Walnut leaves are also galled by the gall mite *Aceria tristriata*, although this species seems to be of very local occurrence. It induces rounded pustules up to 2 mm across. Visible on both leaf surfaces, they usually develop on or close to the veins. Young galls are green, but they later become yellowish and then brown. The mites are almost completely enclosed in the galls, with just a very narrow, hairless opening on the underside.

The gall mite *Eriophyes viburni* is responsible for these hairy pink or red galls on the wayfaring tree. Up to 3 mm across, the galls usually develop on the upper leaf surface, with hairy openings on the underside. They are green in the spring but colour up in the summer. The mites leave the galls in late summer, by which time the galls are mostly brown, and spend the winter in bark crevices. Although found mainly on the wayfaring tree, the mites occasionally affect guelder rose and other related plants.

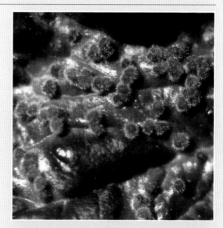

Tightly bunched leaves at the tips of yew shoots are the galls of the gall midge *Taxomyia taxi*. Up to 3 cm tall, each gall supports a single orange or red larva. Most larvae have a two-year life cycle. Eggs are laid on the foliage in late spring and the resulting larvae burrow into the dormant buds, but galls do not develop until the following spring. The larvae then feed for another year before pupating in their galls. A small proportion of larvae complete their lives in twelve months and their galls are smaller, with fewer leaves.

The gall mite *Cecidophyopsis psilaspis* is responsible for this yew gall, which is essentially a swollen bud with fleshy inner leaves. Adult mites overwinter in old galls and lay their eggs there in the spring. The resulting young mites move away to feed in the young buds, but galls develop only if the buds are heavily infested. The galls are fully developed by mid-summer, when they are up to 10 mm long. Several generations of mites are produced in the galls, so a mature gall contains all stages of the life cycle. The mites can also live as inquilines (*see p. 12*) in the galls of *Taxomyia*.

Yellow blisters developing on both leaf surfaces of alexanders in spring and summer are galls of the rust fungus **Puccinia smyrnii**. Also found on the stems, which may become thickened and distorted, the galls bear the aecia of the fungus (*see p. 7*) which produce spores that can infect new plants immediately. Later in the year, dark brown telia develop on the undersides of the leaves and scatter the overwintering teliospores (*see p. 7*). The fungus is generally common, but most frequent in coastal areas.

The gall mite **Cecidophyes nudus** attacks the leaves of both wood avens (pictured here) and water avens, causing prominent puckering of the upper surface.

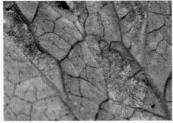

The bulges range from green to red and often cover much of the leaf. The corresponding hollows on the undersides of the leaves are lined with erinea that are initially white but later purplish-grey or brown (*above*). Numerous mites live among the long, slender hairs of the erinea. The galls can be found throughout the year, although the mites may become dormant in the coldest months. Most frequent on the leaf blades, the galls also occur on the petioles and on the flower stalks and sepals.

Lady's bedstraw and, less often, hedge bedstraw are galled by the gall midge **Geocrypta galii**. The galls are smooth, green, reddish, or pinkish swellings at the nodes and they may turn brown as they age. Each gall is more or less globular and contains a single orange larva, but it is quite common for several galls to fuse together and completely encircle the stem. Mature galls open at the side, allowing the larvae to escape and pupate in the soil. There are several generations in a year.

The gall mite *Aceria galiobia* attacks several bedstraw species although in Britain it appears to be most common on lady's bedstraw. It causes the flower buds to swell, especially those at the top of the stem. They commonly assume a conical shape with a rather lumpy or grooved surface, and may reach 10 mm in length. Young galls are green, and those on lady's bedstraw tend to turn brown or black as they mature. Those on hedge bedstraw, pictured here, often remain green even when mature. Maturity is reached in late summer and the adult mites probably spend the winter in the old galls or in the leaf litter.

This greatly swollen flower bud of bird's-foot trefoil is the gall of the gall midge *Contarinia loti*. Galled buds are up to 12 mm long and they do not open. All the enclosed floral organs are swollen. The galls, which can be found throughout the summer months, are green or yellowish at first and become reddish or brown as they mature. Each gall contains several white or yellowish jumping larvae. Mature larvae leave the galls to pupate in the soil and there are two or three generations in a year.

The gall midge *Wachtliella persicariae* is responsible for the severe distortion of these bistort leaves. It sometimes causes no more than rolled and thickened leaf margins, but more often the leaves are completely rolled, as pictured here, and they may also be spirally coiled. The galls are fleshy and quite fragile and, unlike many other leaf rolls, they cannot be unrolled without breaking them. They occur on both common and amphibious bistort and can be found throughout the summer months. Young galls are green and the pink or purple colour gradually develops as they age. Mature galls are often completely purple. Each gall

contains several light red or orange larvae, which pupate in the galls when mature.

Irregular, ribbed swellings in the stems and flower stalks of cat's-ear are galls of the gall wasp **Phanacis hypochoeridis**. Although developing mainly in the stems and flower stalks, the galls sometimes occur in the leaf stalks as well. They develop from mid-summer onwards and are usually 1–5 cm long, containing up to 50 larvae, each in its own little chamber. Soft and green at first, they become brown and often rather wrinkled as they mature in late summer. The insects pupate in the galls in the autumn and remain there until late spring, when the new adults emerge. Although widely distributed on rough grassland in the southern half of the British Isles, this gall is very local and rarely common.

The gall wasp **Xestophanes potentillae** induces galls on creeping cinquefoil, either in the creeping stems or in the underground rootstocks. Galls developing on the rootstocks tend to be globular and often clustered together (*below right*), but those on the aerial stems are usually elongated, pod-like growths up to 2 cm long (*below left*). Galls in both situations contain several larval chambers. Development begins during the summer and in their early stages the aerial galls are pale green and the subterranean ones are cream. They all mature in the autumn, when they generally become orange or light brown. The insects pupate in the galls and new adults emerge in the following spring.

Common cleavers, also called goose-grass, is galled by at least two gall mites of the genus **Cecidophyes**. These cause the edges of the leaves to thicken and roll inwards to enclose the mites in a mass of hairs. Whole leaves are commonly severely distorted, as pictured here. Affected leaves are pale at first, but often become rust-coloured later. For a long time the mite causing the galls in the British Isles was thought to be **Cecidophyes galii**, but recent research has shown that British galls are all caused by **C. rouhollahi**. The galls of the two species are identical.

Galls of the gall midge **Dasineura trifolii** are very common on clovers, especially on white clover, although they are easily overlooked. The insects cause one or more leaflets to fold up along the mid-rib, forming pod-like swellings that vary from green to red or purple. Each gall encloses one or more larvae, which are white at first but become orange as they mature. There are two or three generations in a year. Larvae of the summer generations pupate in the galls, but those of the autumn brood pupate in the soil.

The gall mite **Aceria geranii** attacks bloody cranesbill and other *Geranium* species, causing the terminal leaves to thicken and roll up and bunch together into a loose 'mop', as pictured here. The stem below the galls may also be unusually thick. Galled leaves are pale green or yellowish at first, with the pink or red colour developing later. **A. dolichosoma** induces similar galls on bloody cranesbill, but these galls are noticeably hairy.

The gall midge *Contarinia quinquenotata* is responsible for these swollen day-lily buds. Female midges emerging from their subterranean pupae in spring and early summer lay their eggs in the flower buds. The midge larvae feed in the buds and cause the petals to become thick and distorted, with jagged edges, but the buds do not open. They gradually turn brown and fall, and the mature larvae escape to pupate in the soil. This species arrived in the British Isles from the continent only in the 1980s, but has now spread to many parts of southern England. Late-flowering varieties of day-lily are relatively free from the pest because their buds do not appear until the female midges have finished laying their eggs.

The rust fungus *Melampsora populnea* attacks the leaves of dog's mercury in spring and early summer, causing them to swell and roll up as pictured here. Stems and petioles are also galled and may be greatly distorted. The orange pustules are the aecia of the fungus (*see p. 7*). The fungus also galls pine and larch, where aecia erupt from the needles and from swollen twigs and branches. Later in the year the fungus invades the leaves of poplars, especially white poplar and aspen, where it produces its over-wintering teliospores (*see p. 7*).

Chirosia betuleti, a little grey fly resembling a small house-fly, is responsible for this mop-headed frond of male fern. Eggs are laid in the tip of the frond and the resulting larvae tunnel into the main stalk, causing it to twist and the pinnae (the major divisions of the frond) to become bunched and distorted. Some of the pinnae may turn brown and die. The gall can be found from early summer until late in the autumn and it occurs on lady fern and buckler ferns as well as on male fern. The fly probably spends the winter on the ground in the pupal stage.

Bracken fronds are commonly attacked by the fly *Chirosia grossicauda,* whose larvae tunnel in the central veins of the pinnules (the secondary divisions of the frond) in late summer and cause them to roll downwards from the tip. Mature larvae probably pupate in their galls, but the pupae are likely to fall out as the fronds wither in the autumn, so winter is spent in the pupal stage in the leaf litter on the ground.

The gall midge *Dasineura pteridis* is responsible for these dark swellings on bracken fronds. The edges of the smallest frond divisions (the pinnulets) become rolled and thickened and each roll contains a yellowish larva. Up to 5 mm long, the galls are green at first but eventually become dark brown or black, and usually very shiny – giving rise to the common name of little black pudding galls. The midge has two generations each year and galls can be found throughout the summer and autumn. Mature larvae leave the galls and pupate in the soil, those of the autumn generation remaining in the soil throughout the winter.

The gall wasp *Aulacidea tragopogonis* induces clusters of globular galls at the bases of goat's-beard stems, where they are not easy to find. Occasional galls develop higher up the stems, but these are always smaller and were once thought to be caused by a different species. The galls, which are found mainly in the south-east of Britain, develop in the summer and mature in the autumn. The larvae overwinter in the mature galls and pupate in the spring, with new adults emerging in the summer.

This grossly deformed maize cob has been galled by the fungus *Ustilago maydis*, commonly known as maize smut or corn smut. The fungus can infect all the aerial parts of the plant, but is particularly common in the flower heads. The galls here may be as much as 20 cm in diameter. They are silvery-white at first, but soon become darker and the covering membrane ruptures to expose the dark brown spore mass. The spores remain dormant through the winter, either free in the ground or attached to harvested grain, and after germinating in the spring they usually infect new plants by entering through wounds. Although maize smut can cause severe crop losses, the galls themselves are regarded as a delicacy (huitlacoche) in Central America, which is the original home of the fungus. Maize is actually cultivated in some areas especially for the galls, which can be more valuable than the maize itself. Rich in vitamins and amino acids, they are harvested when young (they become inedible and possibly toxic when the spores turn black) and are used mainly in soups. Good gall crops are readily obtained by sowing maize seeds that have been contaminated with the fungal spores.

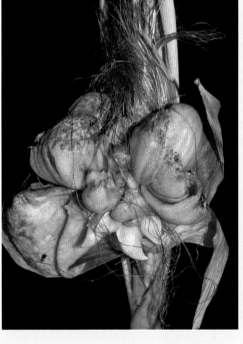

These purplish brown growths emerging from couch grass spikelets are sclerotia of the ascomycete fungus **Claviceps purpurea**, commonly known as ergot. The sclerotia fall to the ground in the autumn and remain dormant until the spring, when they develop fruiting bodies which produce spores that infect another generation of grass flowers. The fungus then destroys the flowers before producing another crop of sclerotia. Many grass species, including rye and other cereals, are attacked by the fungus. The sclerotia are very poisonous and have been responsible for many human deaths when eaten in bread and other cereal products.

The fly **Lipara lucens** is responsible for this cylindrical gall, known as a cigar gall, on common reed. Up to 6 cm long, it consists of a cluster of leaves with a woody central chamber and contains a single fly larva. The galls become brown in autumn and are very conspicuous on the dead stems in the winter. The larvae remain in the dry galls and pupate in the spring, with new adult flies emerging in June.

Ground elder leaves and petioles commonly bear small rounded or oval mounds, which are the galls of the ascomycete fungus ***Protomyces macrosporus***. Visible on both leaf surfaces, the galls are pale yellow or almost colourless and translucent. They can be found from early in the summer until the leaves die down with the autumn frosts. As the galls mature, sections of the fungal threads inside them develop thick walls and turn into resting spores that survive the winter. These spores germinate in the spring, producing another type of spore called an endospore. The endospores fuse in pairs and produce hyphae that invade new ground elder leaves.

The rust fungus ***Puccinia glechomatis*** galls the leaves of ground-ivy, producing these prominent yellow swellings on the undersides of the leaves. Up to 4 mm across, these galls develop during the summer and gradually become dotted with the telia (*see p. 7*). The latter produce dense clusters of thick-walled teliospores, which are orange at first, as pictured here, but gradually become dark brown. The teliospores remain dormant through the winter and germinate in the spring, when they produce wind-blown spores that infect fresh leaves. Galls can also develop on the stems.

These attractive galls on the leaves of ground-ivy are caused by the gall wasp ***Liposthenes glechomae***. Whole leaves may be converted into the hairy spheres, each of which usually contains a single larva. Galls also develop on the stems and leaf stalks. Young galls are green or yellowish and some, especially in shady places, stay like this. Galls can be found throughout the summer, but as they mature in the autumn they become pale grey. The larvae pupate in the galls and new adults emerge in late spring. Fresh galls have a pleasant, minty smell and were apparently eaten by French peasants at one time.

Known as the light-house gall because of its beacon-like red tip when mature, this gall is caused by the gall midge **Rondaniola bursaria** and is common on ground-ivy leaves in the summer. Up to 4 mm tall, each gall contains a single larva. The galls fall in late summer, leaving neat round holes in the leaves. They remain on the ground throughout the winter and the larvae pupate inside them. New adults emerge in the spring and the females lay their eggs on the young ground ivy leaves to start the cycle again.

This groundsel stem (*below left*) has been galled by the rust fungus **Puccinia lagenophorae** which can cause severe distortion of both stems and leaves. The orange patches bear the aecia, which appear as cup-like structures under high magnification and bear aeciospores on their margins (*see p. 7*). These spores can infect new plants directly. Dark telia (*see p. 7*) occur among the aecia in the autumn (*below right*). The fungus, which is a native of Australia and known in Britain only since 1961, also attacks Oxford ragwort.

The gall wasp **Aulacidea hieracii** is responsible for rounded or elongated galls, up to 4 cm long, on hawkweeds (*below*). Green and often rather hairy at first, the galls darken as they mature in the autumn. Each gall houses numerous larvae, which remain in the galls through the winter and pupate in the spring.

These hemp agrimony stems have been galled by the caterpillars of *Adaina microdactyla*, which is the smallest of our plume moths: its feathery wings span no more than 17 mm. Galls usually develop as irregular swellings in or close to the nodes and galled plants can often be recognised by the drooping of the upper shoots and flowers. When the caterpillars are active the gall openings are marked by accumulations of droppings. Once feeding has stopped, the droppings fall away to reveal the small, circular openings. Pupation occurs in the stems just below the galls and there are two generations each year, with adult insects on the wing in May and June and again in August.

This hollyhock leaf has been galled by the rust fungus *Puccinia malvacearum*, which also attacks the stems and leaf stalks. The hard, orange swellings will later become powdery as the teliospores (*see p. 7*) erupt from the surface. Most of the teliospores germinate straight away and produce wind-blown spores that spread the infection. Other teliospores overwinter on the dead leaves or in the soil and germinate in the spring. Heavy infestations can cause severe distortion and even death of the leaves. Various mallows are also attacked by this fungus.

The gall mite *Aceria labiatiflorae* galls the terminal parts of marjoram shoots, causing both flowers and leaves to become thick and distorted and clothed with mats of white hairs. Nothing else appears to be known of the mite's life cycle or overwintering habits.

These bright orange swellings on meadowsweet leaves are the aecia (*see p. 7*) of the rust fungus ***Triphragmium ulmariae***. Developing mainly on the leaf veins and petioles, the galls can be seen mainly in early summer and affected leaves may become severely distorted. Dark, resting teliospores (*see p. 7*) can be found on the undersides of the leaves towards the end of the summer and well into the autumn.

The gall midge ***Dasineura ulmaria*** induces these smooth red pimples on the upper surfaces of meadowsweet leaves. The galls are up to 2 mm in diameter and they usually develop on the veins. They open on the undersides of the leaves by way of tubular or spiky and rather hairy yellowish projections. Each gall contains a single pale yellow larva, which pupates in the gall when mature. There are two or three generations in a year and galls can be found throughout the summer months.

The gall midge ***Dasineura pustulans*** induces fairly simple galls on meadowsweet leaves early in the summer. Each gall is a small blister on the upper leaf surface, surrounded by a pale yellowish green patch about 5 mm in diameter. Below the blister is a shallow depression containing a single cream or white larva. The latter matures during the summer and falls to the ground to pupate.

The aphid *Cryptosiphum artemisiae* galls the leaves of mugwort, causing part or all of the blade to curl downwards and enclose the dull greyish brown aphids. Young leaves, especially those at the tips of the shoots, often cluster tightly together, as pictured here. Affected leaf areas become thick and often turn red or purple. The aphids breed asexually in the galls for much of the year, but winter is passed in the egg stage.

Mugwort leaves are galled by several other arthropods, including....

...the gall mite *Aceria artemisiae*, which causes somewhat warty, rounded brown or reddish pimples on the uppersides of the leaves. Up to 2 mm high, the galls are sometimes stalked and may be clothed with white hairs. There is a small, hair-ringed opening on the underside of the leaf. The gall midge *Rhopalomyia foliorum* also induces pimples on the uppersides of the leaves. These are normally red or yellow but they are usually ovoid and hairless and they open on the upper leaf surface.

Swellings in the upper parts of mugwort stems are likely to be the galls of the fly *Campiglossa misella.* This is one of the picture-winged flies, so called because the wings are ornately decorated (*see p. 8*). The gall is open at the top and the shoot above it normally withers away. Each gall contains several white larvae in late spring and early summer. Pupation takes place in the gall and the new adults lay their eggs in the flower heads, where the next brood of larvae feed without inducing galls. The insects pass the winter as dormant adults.

The rust fungus *Puccinia lapsanae* attacks nipplewort leaves, especially those of seedling plants in the spring, producing these reddish blisters and often causing marked distortion of both blade and petiole. The blisters, which may develop on both sides of the leaf, eventually bear orange aecia (*see p. 7*) whose spores can immediately infect new plants. Later in the year the leaves bear tiny, dark telia (*see p. 7*), the teliospores from which remain dormant in the soil through the winter and infect new plants when they germinate in the spring.

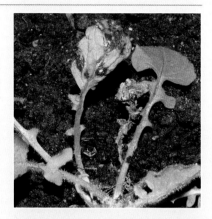

This common orache plant has been galled by the waxy, yellowish-green aphid *Hayhurstia atriplicis*. The leaf blades become thick and roll upwards at the edges to enclose the aphids in pod-like chambers, and may also develop bulges along the mid-rib. The leaf stalks often become contorted as well and all affected areas generally become distinctly pale or yellowish before turning brown as the galls mature. Galls containing asexual winged and wingless aphids can be found in all but the coldest months of the year. Sexual forms appear in the autumn and, after mating, the wingless females lay their overwintering eggs on the stems. The insect is commonly known as the boat-gall aphid in America because of the shape of its galls.

The gall wasp *Aylax papaveris* galls the seed capsules of the field poppy and the long-headed poppy. The capsule of the latter is often much enlarged (as seen here) and the stalk may become twisted. Galling is less obvious in the field poppy, although the capsule is slightly enlarged and distorted. The gall tissue may fill the capsule entirely, enclosing many larval chambers and leaving little room for the seeds. The galls mature in late summer and the insects pupate in the galls. New adults emerge in the following spring.

The gall midge *Asphondylia ononidis* is responsible for this gall on common restharrow. The galls are either swollen pods or enlarged stipules at the leaf bases (as pictured here) and, in common with other *Asphondylia* galls, they are lined with a fungal mycelium (*see p. 38*). Each gall contains a single yellow larva. The larvae pupate in their galls and there are two generations each year. On the continent, the midge also induces galls on spiny restharrow.

Rockroses are commonly galled by the gall midge *Dasineura helianthemi*, whose larvae cause the terminal leaves to become thick and hairy. Affected leaves also curl inwards and enclose the orange larvae in a type of 'artichoke' gall. The galls mature at the end of the summer and the larvae then leave to pupate in the soil, producing new adults in the following spring.

The psyllid *Livia junci* attacks the flowering spikes of several kinds of rush, causing the floral parts to become thick and leaf-like and to form what is commonly known as a tassel gall. Each cluster may be as much as 8 cm across and may contain up to 80 spikelets, each surrounding a single psyllid nymph. Inhabited galls can be found from June until well into the autumn. They are red at first, but they turn brown as they mature. Adult psyllids leave the galls in the autumn and spend the winter, probably in dormant state, on the basal parts of the rushes. Eggs are laid in the flower buds in the spring to begin the cycle again. Galled shoots tend to be thick and stunted and shorter than unaffected shoots, so the galls are not always easy to spot.

Albugo candida is responsible for this crusty coating on shepherd's purse. Although fungus-like, it belongs to a different kingdom – the Chromista – and is one of a small group known as blister rusts that may cause thickening and distortion of stems, leaves, and fruits. The white coating consists of masses of shiny spore capsules that burst through the plant's epidermis. The organism attacks a wide range of cruciferous plants and can cause severe damage to cultivated brassicas. The downy mildew

Peronospora parasitica also forms a white coating on many crucifers but, unlike those of *Albugo*, its spore-bearing threads are soft and fluffy.

Circular blisters on sow-thistle leaves are galls of the gall midge **Cystiphora sonchi**. Typically 4–5 mm in diameter, each gall has a pale centre surrounded by a purple or reddish ring, and its position is marked on the underside of the leaf by a slight concavity. Each gall accommodates a yellowish larva. There are two or three broods in a year, with summer insects pupating in the galls. Larvae maturing in the autumn pupate in the soil. Although

most common on smooth sow-thistle, galls can also be found on perennial and prickly sow-thistles.

Germander speedwell is very commonly galled by the gall midge **Jaapiella veronicae**, which attacks the shoot tips and causes the two terminal pairs of leaves to cling tightly together and form a hairy pouch. Each pouch contains numerous orange larvae. There are several generations in a year, with larvae of the summer broods pupating in the galls. Autumn larvae leave the galls and overwinter in the soil before pupating in the spring.

The stems and leaves of stinging nettles commonly bear conspicuous orange or reddish swellings caused by the rust fungus *Puccinia urticata*. These galls bear the aecia of the fungus (*see p. 7*), which shed spores that infect other nettles or else move on to various sedges, where the telial stage of the life cycle (*see p. 7*) occurs without inducing galls. Different sedges are host to different varieties  of this rust, eleven of which occur in Britain. Strictly host-limited, these varieties are not distinguishable in the aecial stage on nettles.

These swellings on stinging nettle leaves are the galls of the gall midge *Dasineura urticae*. Individual galls are up to 8 mm in diameter but neighbouring galls often fuse together. Ranging from green to purple, each gall contains one or more white larvae. Mature larvae leave the galls through mouth-like slits on the upper surface and pupate in the soil. There are probably  two or three generations in a year. Galls also occur, less frequently, on the stems.

The psyllid *Trioza urticae* galls stinging nettle leaves, normally attacking young leaves at the tips of the shoots. Affected leaves exhibit a number of small pimples on the upper surface, with corresponding hollows underneath. Each hollow accommodates a psyllid nymph. Heavily infested leaves become stunted and crinkled and often much darker than the unaffected foliage, as pictured here. There are two or three generations in a year and galled plants are usually most obvious in late summer when the psyllid populations are at their peak. Insects maturing in the autumn leave the nettles to spend the winter months in turf or in various evergreen shrubs.

The gall midge **Rhopalomyia tanaceticola** induces egg-shaped or vase-like galls on tansy. Up to 10 mm high, the galls develop in the leaf axils, on the leaves (*above left*), or in the flower heads (*above right*), and when fully developed the apex is noticeably lobed or toothed. Each gall accommodates a single pink or orange larva, which pupates in the gall when mature. There are two or more broods in a year and galls can be found throughout the summer, although those on the foliage are not easy to spot.

These large swellings in the stems of creeping thistle are galls of the fly **Urophora cardui**, which is one of the picture-winged flies (*see p. 8*). Up to 10 cm long, the galls gradually become brown and woody as they mature in late summer. Each contains one or more larval chambers and the larvae remain in the galls when the plants die down in the autumn. They pupate in the spring, but new

adult flies cannot emerge until the galls start to rot and disintegrate. They normally emerge in mid-summer and lay their eggs in the tips of young shoots. Common in southern areas, the gall seems to have extended its range into the northern half of England in recent years. The species is absent from Ireland.

Wild thyme is commonly galled by the gall mite *Aceria thomasi*, which causes the terminal leaves to bunch up and form more or less globular rosettes up to 10 mm in diameter. Each gall is covered with long white hairs, amongst which the mites live and feed, and heavily infested carpets of thyme look entirely white from a distance. Inhabited galls can be found throughout the summer. Little seems to be known of the life history of this mite.

The gall midge *Contarinia craccae* is responsible for these attractive lantern-shaped galls on tufted vetch. Each gall is a swollen flower bud and each contains several jumping larvae that are white at first and then pale orange. Affected flowers do not open and the galls are gradually hollowed out by the developing larvae. Mature larvae leave the galls and pupate in the soil. There are probably two generations in a year.

The gall midge *Dasineura viciae* attacks various vetches, especially the common vetch and bush vetch, causing the leaflets to swell and fold up to form pod-like galls. These often form dense clusters ranging from green, through yellow to red and reaching 40 mm in diameter. Each pod may contain several white larvae, which leave to pupate in the soil when fully grown. There are two or three generations in a year.

These sweet violet leaves have been galled by the gall midge **Dasineura odoratae** (*see p. 8*). When mature leaves are attacked their margins thicken, usually in the basal half (*right, above*), and roll upwards to form pouches in which the larvae live and feed. The galls are usually rather hairy and affected leaves are quite conspicuous. If young leaves are attacked they generally roll up completely, forming solid-looking structures that do not look like leaves at all (*right, below*). White at first, the larvae become pale orange as they mature. Many individuals live in each gall and there are several generations in a year. Pupation takes place inside the galls. *Dasineura odoratae* appears to be confined to the southern half of Britain and is absent from Ireland but **Dasineura affinis**, which induces similar galls on dog violets, is a much more widely distributed species.

This violet petiole, towards the right of the picture, has been attacked by the smut fungus **Urocystis violae**, which also affects the leaf veins and rootstocks. The fungus galls many species of violet, including their garden cultivars. Infected organs thicken noticeably as the fungus develops inside them and then develop blister-like swellings, from which dark brown masses of powdery spores are eventually released. Galled organs can often be found during the winter.

The gall midge *Jaapiella bryoniae* is responsible for distorting the shoot tips of white bryony in the summer. The galls consist of swollen young leaves and flower buds clustered together in a hairy mass that may be as much as 30 mm in diameter. Each gall contains numerous white larvae, which leave to pupate in the soil when mature. The very similar *Jaapiella parvula* galls individual flower buds, causing them to swell up and turn brown. Galled buds do not open and they fall from the plants before the unaffected flowers have completed their development.

The gall midge *Kiefferia pericarpiicola* galls wild carrot plants, usually attacking the developing fruits and converting them into the thick-walled pouches pictured here. Young galls are greenish yellow and hard to spot in the flower-heads. The galls, which can be found in late summer and autumn, are up to 5 mm in diameter and each contains a single orange larva. Mature larvae leave their galls to pupate in the soil, where the insects pass the winter. Galls of this midge can also be found on other umbelliferous plants, including burnet saxifrage, and sometimes develop on the flower stalks instead of in the fruits.

These swellings on the stems of rosebay willowherb are galls of the moth *Mompha sturnipennella*. The galls appear early in the summer and are most noticeable in the side shoots and the upper parts of the main stems. Although possibly more common lower down in the stems, the swellings are less obvious there. Each gall contains a single caterpillar, which pupates in a cocoon in or on the soil and produces a new adult moth in July. Summer adults lay their eggs in the seed pods or in the slender upper shoots and are said not to form galls, although inhabited galls have been found in the upper shoots until well into the autumn. The insect overwinters in the adult state.

The leaves of rosebay willowherb commonly exhibit thickened and tightly down-rolled margins. These are the galls of the gall midge *Dasineura kiefferiana*. Individual galls are up to 10 mm long and contain a single yellowish larva, although neighbouring galls often join together and the galls then appear to contain several larvae. Mature larvae leave to pupate in the soil and there may be more than one generation in a year.

Wood sage is frequently galled by the rust fungus **Puccinia annularis**, which is responsible for the dark brown pustules that occur on the undersides of the leaves during the summer and autumn. These spots, which vary in size, bear the telia (*see p. 7*). Slightly concave at first, they gradually swell into domed clusters and scatter teliospores that germinate without any dormant period. This rust has no other spore-bearing stages and no other host plant, passing its entire life cycle on wood sage. Very similar galls have recently been found on the ornamental tree germander (*Teucrium fruticans*) and have been referred to the closely related *Puccinia teucrii*.

The gall midge **Rhopalomyia millefolii** is responsible for these attractive little galls on yarrow. The galls normally develop in axillary buds, but also occur on the leaves and occasionally on the flowers. Rounded at first (*right, above*), they gradually open into bell-shaped structures up to 10 mm long with markedly hairy lobes around the margin (*right, below*), but they are still quite difficult to spot amongst the densely-packed foliage. Each gall contains a single yellow larva. Young galls are green and shiny and those exposed to the sun may turn deep red for a while. All galls become glossy brown as they mature. There are two or more broods in a year, with summer larvae pupating in their galls. Autumn-maturing larvae leave their galls and pupate in the soil.

Further Reading

The following books will enable the enthusiast to name many of our galls and will also provide a good deal of background information on their natural history. The newer publications contain numerous references that will guide the reader further into the mysterious and fascinating world of cecidology. It is also well worth tracking down some of the older books through the library system. Many names will have changed, but numerous fascinating snippets of biology can be found in these ancient tomes.

CONNOLD, E. T. 1901 *British Vegetable Galls* Hutchinson

CONNOLD, E. T. 1908 *British Oak Galls* Adlard

CONNOLD, E. T. 1909 *Plant Galls of Great Britain* Adlard

DARLINGTON, A. 1968 *The Pocket Encyclopaedia of Plant Galls in Colour* Blandford

MALPIGHI, M. 1679 *De Gallis – On Galls* A Facsimile together with a Translation and Interpretation by Margaret Redfern, Alexander J. Cameron, and Kevin Down. 2008, The Ray Society, London

RANDOLPH, S. 2005 *The Natural History of the Rose Bedeguar Gall* BPGS

REDFERN, M. 2011 *Plant Galls* Collins (New Naturalist No. 117)

REDFERN, M., SHIRLEY, P. & BLOXHAM, M. 2011 *British Plant Galls* Field Studies Council [a revised version of the authors' 2002 keys first published in *Field Studies* **10**, 207-531]

REDFERN, M. & ASKEW, R. R. 1992 *Plant Galls* Naturalists' Handbook **17** Richmond Publishing Co.

SWANTON, E. W. 1912 *British Plant Galls* Methuen

WILLIAMS, R. 2009 *Oak-Galls in Britain* [Vols I & II: revised edition] Vanellus Publications

The following continental publications will be useful for anyone planning to look for galls on the European mainland.

BELLMANN, H. 2012 *Geheimnisvolle Pflanzengallen* Quelle & Meyer (in German)

CSÓKA, G. 1996 *Gubacsok (Plant Galls)* Forest Research Institute, Budapest (in Hungarian and English)

DAUPHIN, P. 2012 *Guide des Galles de France et d'Europe* Belin (in French)

KOOPS, R.J. 2013 *Veldgids Plantengallen* (in Dutch)

LAMBINON, J. CARBONNELLE, S. & CLAEREBOUT, S. 2015 *Aide-mémoire de cécidologie: Choix de zoocécidies de la Belgique* (in French)

ROSKAM, H. C. 2009 *W. M. Docters van Leeuwen: Gallenboek.* [4th edition: revised and adapted by H. C. Roskam] KNNV Uitgeverij [in Dutch]

Acknowledgements

Michael Chinery would like to thank the following members of the British Plant Gall Society for their help and encouragement throughout the planning and preparation of this book: Jerry Bowdrey, Rex Hancy, Keith Harris, Tom Higginbottom, Joe Ostojá-Starzewski, Tom Preece, Margaret Redfern, Peter Shirley, and Brian Spooner, all of who have contributed material and/or read the scripts and made valuable comments and suggestions. Particular thanks go to Chris Leach, who suggested that the Society should produce the book in the first place and also gave much support throughout the process.

The following photographers have kindly allowed us to reproduce their images in the book. The images are listed by page numbers and then the position on the page – top, centre, bottom, left and right.

Martyn Ainsworth 70(t)

Jojanneke Bijkerk 38(b), 39(b), 55(t), 67(b), 71(c), 75(b), 83 (c)(b), 88(c)(b)

Bert Brand 89(b)

Peter Cooke 45(t), 48(c), 49(b), 63(t), 92(t)

Gyuri Csóka 16(b), 19(b), 24(t), 56(t), 67(t), 86(t)

Brian Ecott 26 (t)(c)

Hewett Ellis 60(b)

Ian Farmer 79(bl), 85(t), 91(b)

Maggie Frankum 20(c)

Rex Hancy 15(b), 25(b), 36(b), 53(b), 73(c)

Keith Harris 38(c), 61(t)

Tom Higginbottom 5(b), 7(tr), 16(c),17(bl), 21(t), 24(b), 25(t), 27, 31(c)(b), 32(c), 35(t), 37(t)(c), 41(tr), 45(b), 50(b), 55(b)(c), 60(c), 62 (b), 63(b), 64(t), 65(b), 74(b), 75(c), 77(tr), 81(t), 90(t)

Roelof Jan Koops 7(tl), 22(inset), 40(c), 54(t), 59(b), 71(b), 84(b), 85(b)

Marcela Skuhravá 84(t)

Len Worthington 11(tr), 23(tr), 32(t), 35(c), 60(t), 66(t), 80(b), 84(c), 88(t)

Most of the other photographs are by Michael Chinery, but there are a few images for which, despite diligent searches through the Society's archives, we have been unable to trace the photographers. Please accept our apologies for these omissions.

Index of Host Plants

THE BRITISH PLANT GALL SOCIETY

The British Plant Gall Society was formed in 1985 in response to the growing interest in the study of plant galls, their causers, and their other inhabitants. Although called the British Plant Gall Society, the Society's interests are by no means confined to the British Isles and it aims to bring together cecidologists, both amateur and professional, from all over the world. The Society already has strong links with gall enthusiasts in The Netherlands and its first international meeting was held on Dutch soil in 2009. Another International Meeting was held in Belgium in 2015.

Membership is open to anyone with an interest in plant galls and members include universities and research institutes as well as individual naturalists. These members have widely different backgrounds and interests, covering a broad spectrum of biological disciplines ranging from basic natural history and ecology to molecular biology and the relatively new subject of gene sequencing.

The Society's AGM is held during a residential weekend, allowing members to make friends and swap information as well as to gather galls and expand our knowledge of their ecology and distribution. The event is based in a different area each year, so participants get to see galls from a wide range of habitats. The Society's regional representatives also organise a full programme of field meetings in various parts of the country each year. Regular workshops are organised for members wishing to learn more about the insects and other invertebrates living in the galls.

The Society's illustrated journal, *Cecidology*, is published twice a year, in spring and autumn, and carries a variety of academic papers as well as anecdotal contributions and records of notable discoveries. The Society has produced several other publications, including keys to facilitate the identification of all known British galls (*see p. 92*), and members are continually contributing to a computerised recording scheme that will permit the production of detailed distribution maps for many British galls. An extensive library of digital and film images is at the disposal of members wishing to give talks on galls and their inhabitants..

Details of all BPGS meetings and other activities, together with information on joining the Society, can be found on the Society's website – **www.britishplantgallsociety.org**.